J. WESTON
WALCH
PUBLISHER

Second Edition

World History
on the Screen

Film and Video Resource

Wendy S. Wilson & Gerald H. Herman

User's Guide
to
Walch Reproducible Books

Purchasers of this book are granted the right to reproduce all pages.

This permission is limited to a single teacher, for classroom use only.

Any questions regarding this policy or requests to purchase further reproduction rights should be addressed to

Permissions Editor
J. Weston Walch, Publisher
321 Valley Street • P.O. Box 658
Portland, Maine 04104-0658

Cover photograph © Wide World Photo

Ben Kingsley as Gandhi

1   2   3   4   5   6   7   8   9   10

ISBN 0-8251-4615-1

Copyright © 1990, 2003
J. Weston Walch, Publisher
P.O. Box 658 • Portland, Maine 04104-0658
walch.com

Printed in the United States of America

CONTENTS

Contents

Teacher Introduction

"It is like writing history with lightning!"

Woodrow Wilson exclaimed this in 1915, upon viewing D. W. Griffith's film *The Birth of a Nation.* Today, we are fairly blasé about films and television programs that have, or purport to have, themes based on historical subjects. Yet it is an accepted fact today that, for many people, these media provide their only glimpse of history outside a formal classroom. For our students, films and television provide a chief source of entertainment. Sadly, in many cases students unblinkingly accept what they see on the screen as absolute fact.

With this in mind, it is our purpose to present some sample films you can tie to a world history curriculum, along with some ideas about using the films in the most productive way possible. We hope they will also serve in a broader context, by stimulating media awareness and critical-viewing skills in your students and by turning "media-passive" students into "media-active" students—those who see the viewing of a film not as a comfortable break from classroom work, but as a lesson in critical analysis and historical interpretation.

To do this, we must look at ways in which films can be used in the history classroom. Students are taught to analyze historical documents; a film can be analyzed and studied in much the same way. Several major questions can be asked of the film document: What is the content of the film? What information does it convey or portray? How is the information affected or determined by the necessity to entertain as well as instruct? What influences were at work during the production of the film (e.g., censorship, monetary constraints, attitudes of society, background of producers)? How was the film received when it was released? This is not to say that films should not be enjoyed; however, we must employ a bit of caution in the process. We must teach our students that, in print and film, there is no such thing as a completely objective and unbiased historical account.

The films chosen for this book are presentations of history rather than documentations of history. That is, they are reenactments of historical events rather than documentary records of events, such as a newsreel or actuality footage. These historical-presentation films may present historical content in four ways:

1. **As a factual record:** It is possible to use film to dramatize what has happened in the past. Some directors are very concerned about portraying historical events accurately; Richard Attenborough's *A Bridge Too Far* (1977), Michael Mann's *The Insider* (1999), and Roger Donaldson's *Thirteen Days* (2000) are examples. Occasionally, historians act as advisers or even participate in the production of such films. A good example of this is Natalie Zemon Davis's participation in the making of *The Return of Martin Guerre* (1982).

2. **To convey atmosphere:** It is common for history teachers to use fiction to convey a sense of the past—lifestyles, values, or beliefs. Filmmakers spend much money, time, and energy to make historical presentations—whether fact-based, fictional, or docudramatic (combining elements of each)—look real. Costumes, sets, weapons, and props are often carefully reconstructed to lend legitimacy to the production. For example, in the movie *Cromwell,* the set of the king's court in St. James's Palace is modeled

on the court as shown in paintings of that time period. Seventeenth-century weapons, uniforms, and methods of fighting are accurately portrayed, even if individual events may be distorted.

3. **Analogy:** Occasionally, media producers use a historical event to point out or explain contemporary motives or actions, particularly when the contemporary event is controversial. For example, *Khartoum* (1966) was meant to show not only what happened to Pasha Gordon as the result of the inactivity and indecisiveness of the British government, but also that Americans were risking the same fate through their weak stance on Vietnam. In much the same way, many of the best science-fiction films, from *2001: A Space Odyssey* to the original *Planet of the Apes* (both released in 1968), are meant to be allegories, illuminating contemporary issues by analogy.

4. **As a lesson in historiography:** Because the dramatic form used in films requires consistent, relatively simple motivational interpretations, students can often learn how the time period in which a film has been made interprets historical (and, by implication, contemporary) personalities or events. The interest during the 1960s in pop psychology is evident in *The Lion in Winter* (1968), for instance, although the setting is twelfth-century France. It is particularly in this last framework for studying film that you can use class discussion to encourage students to become more sophisticated in understanding the complex relationship between fact and historical interpretation.

Media resources have expanded dramatically in recent years, with new titles available every month. The films selected for this volume are readily available in videocassette form as well as DVD, in many cases. Many are currently popular with world history teachers. There is also a list of other appropriate films for each unit. Since the distribution of videotapes and DVDs changes frequently, a bibliography of media sources is included to help you check on availability. More and more films are becoming available on DVD, which provides teachers with some advantages. Many DVDs contain ancillary materials such as outtakes, newsreel footage from the time period of the film, or interviews with historical consultants. When a DVD player is interfaced through a computer, there are often hotlinks that lead directly to web sites on related topics. If a computer interface is not possible, teachers can simply copy down the URLs from the DVD and use them on a separate computer to do web research. As the technology changes, films and other video resources are becoming easier and easier for teachers to use. The ability to freeze an image, rewind, and replay a section of a film is much easier than in the past.

Since so many current films with historical subjects are R-rated, technology also makes it easy to skip scenes that may be objectionable. It is recommended that teachers use a permission slip when planning to show R-rated films, even if students are over 17 years old. Also, it is not essential in many cases to show an entire film. Most movies lend themselves to sampling; you can select the scenes most appropriate to your classroom lessons. This is particularly true for very long films, such as *Gandhi* or *Germinal*.

Reproducible student material contained in this book includes A Student Introduction to Historical Films (page *xi*), a Film Analysis Guide Sheet (Appendix A), the Wannsee Protocol (Appendix B), and a Glossary of Common Film Terms (page 155). Most units also include reproducible student pages consisting of a film viewing guide and a worksheet that includes a list of key vocabulary and questions based on the film. We suggest that you hand out both the Film Analysis Guide Sheet and the unit's reproducible pages to students before they view a particular film. The vocabulary lists refer specifically to important terms used in the film or in the introductory materials provided in the unit. You can review the terms with students before they watch the film, or you can have students define them for homework or class work. Likewise, you can determine how to use the worksheet questions—as an in-class written assignment, a springboard for class discussion, or an enrichment assignment to be completed at home.

Finally, we also need to remind our students that movies are produced primarily as vehicles for entertainment. Actors and actresses are generally chosen because they are attractive to the audience. Their characters may have fought in a battle, but their hair is usually clean and their teeth are sparkling white. In their film of seventeenth-century England, *Winstanley* (1975), directors Kevin Brownlow and Andrew Mollo sought to present an accurate image of life at that time. The directors hired amateur actors with careworn faces, matted hair, and bad teeth. Costumes were worn for the duration of the shooting without being laundered, and cast members did not engage in modern hygiene. The comment from most students on viewing this film is "Yuck!" It is important to explain to students that life in the past was not as

clean, manicured, and beautifully coiffured as is usually portrayed by Hollywood. It is also important to explain that, just because a film presents history inaccurately, it does not mean that it is a bad film. *Braveheart* (1999) won an Academy Award® for Best Picture, but it is not an accurate portrayal of thirteenth-century Scotland or the events of that time. (An interesting side note is that *Braveheart* is credited with inspiring the Scottish Nationalist Movement, when it was first shown in Scotland to cheering audiences.) Even a film that has doubtful value as a historical resource can have an important impact on viewers.

We hope that you will find ways to use films as positive teaching tools that provide an active viewing experience for your classes. In our role as social studies teachers, we now need to add critical-viewing skills (or visual literacy) to the list of important abilities our students need to develop for life in our media-conscious society.

A Layperson's Note on Copyright and Fair Use

Copyright is a delicate balancing effort: the federal government wants, on the one hand, to encourage intellectual and artistic creativity by ensuring a fair return for an artist's efforts (as well as profit-engendered distribution systems), while, on the other, to provide an environment in which these ideas and achievements can spread widely to be judged in public review and analysis. Educators have long relied on the doctrine of "fair use" to permit them to use copyrighted materials in their classrooms without prior authorization. The Copyright Law of 1976 substantially circumscribed the concept of fair use, while the results of the author-user conference that accompanied the law's development suggested specific guidelines of brevity, spontaneity, and "cumulative effect"—that is, the extent to which the use interferes with the author's potential market—to help determine whether projected use of copyrighted material is permissible under the law. Both because this was a compromise between users and authors, and because the law attempted to encompass the range of print and electronic media invented since the 1905 law, these guidelines were necessarily vague. Subsequent amendments and additions to the law, such as the Digital Millennium Copyright Act of 1998 and the Sonny Bono Copyright Term Extension Act of 1998, have done little to lend clarity to the situation. The new nonprint media have been an area of particular contention between authors and users, partly because of their ephemeral nature and ease of broadcasting, and partly because of the threat posed to producers and distributors by the explosion in the availability and ease of duplication technologies.

The law in this area is still developing, and definitive conclusions are not yet possible. When films, tapes, or discs are purchased or rented from legitimate educational distributors, specific use licenses accompany them. Beyond this, it is probably legal to use other commercial tapes legitimately acquired by purchase, rental, or lease in direct face-to-face instruction, though not to broadcast them over closed-circuit, instructional, or broadcast radio or television systems or to "digitize" and send them over the Web without a specific license to do so. It is probably illegal to deposit them in libraries for casual listening or viewing, to play them publicly to general (even student) or paying audiences, or to use "pirated" tapes for these purposes. Copies made without permission from other tapes, films, or other recordings are, except for limited preservation purposes, considered pirated copies, even if the recordings from which they were obtained are legitimate.

Under certain circumstances, "off-air" copies may also be legally employed in this same face-to-face instruction for a very limited time before they must be erased, though these should probably be recorded at the site of their proposed "time-shifted" use. ("Off-air" recording means the recording of a televised program, such as a PBS documentary. "Time-shifted" use is the showing of a recorded videotape at a time to suit an individual's need, such as conforming to a specific class meeting time.) To facilitate such use, many educational distributors are offering to license such recordings for educational purposes for a set time or for "the life of the tape" as an alternative to more expensive rentals or purchases. In addition, specialized off-air and commercial copy-licensing clearinghouses are now in existence or are being formed.

The legitimacy of excerpting unauthorized clips or cuts for summary presentation, review, or critical analysis remains an open question (those seen or heard on television or radio previews or review programs are provided by the distributors for this use), and many areas of nonprint media use remain murky or undefined. It is therefore important to consult some of the many guides available from professional organizations, clearinghouses, or copyright experts and to seek legal advice (often available at the district level or through the local superintendent's office) when the fact or situation of the proposed media use raises questions or poses special problems.

A Student Introduction to Historical Films

You have probably heard the expressions "Seeing is believing" and "A picture is worth a thousand words." It may seem to you that a truthful, and certainly enjoyable, way to learn history is through pictures—moving pictures, or films. It is true that films do provide us with presentations of historical events, such as the Vietnam War or the French Revolution. Historical themes have been popular as long as motion pictures have been produced. It is also true, however, that films provide us with *interpretations* of historical personalities and events. Just as you have learned to be critical of print documents, you must bring that same critical eye to nonprint or media documents. It is important to learn critical-viewing skills to use when you see media productions in your social studies classes, on television at home, or at the movies.

In order to take full advantage of the films you see, you should ask several major questions while viewing:

1. What is the content of the film? What information does it convey?

2. How and/or why was the film produced? What forces were at work during its production that might have affected its final form? (For example: Censorship? Background of the producers? Budgetary limitations?)

3. How was the film received when it came out? Was it popular? Did it have any effect on the attitudes of the people who saw it?

Films are produced first of all to entertain and, perhaps, second of all to instruct. Therefore, it is important to remember that few film producers are willing to risk the box-office draw of their film for historical accuracy. If a choice is to be made between entertainment and historical fact, the truth may suffer. Why, then, use a film for learning at all? Why not use print materials alone, such as textbooks and readings?

First, print materials, like films, must be interpreted and analyzed carefully for historical accuracy. Next, films can be a valuable way to go back through time to

(continued)

experience the atmosphere of a past era or to "see" historical characters long dead. Many film production companies try very hard to make the settings for their historical presentations as accurate as possible. They employ historians as consultants to advise in the construction of sets, costume design, weaponry, transportation, manners, and other details. Sometimes historians play an even more central role. A good example of this is the film *The Return of Martin Guerre* (1982). Natalie Zemon Davis, author of the book that inspired the movie and former president of the American Historical Association, worked on the production. The film thus provides a very accurate portrayal of rural peasant life in the sixteenth century. (However, Professor Davis was disappointed that the characters were presented in ways to make the film more entertaining and appealing to a modern audience.)

Other films are less true to history; they are designed primarily for entertainment, with little regard for fact. The best example of this is the Academy Award®-winning movie *Braveheart* (1995). William Wallace was a real person who lived between 1272 and 1305 in Scotland, and he did lead the Scottish war for independence from England. Other than the grisly method of his execution, little else portrayed in this film is historically true. The real Wallace was a knight who wore battle armor and never would have worn a kilt. He lived in a substantial house, not an earthen mound. Is *Braveheart* a good film? Certainly it is very entertaining. When first shown in Scotland, it caused audiences to jump to their feet and join the actors in shouting "Freedom! Freedom!" Membership in the Scottish National Party (or SNP) rose dramatically after *Braveheart* finished its run in Scottish movie theaters. It is an exciting, well-acted film with entertainment value. It is not accurate history, though, nor was it probably meant to be.

When you watch films in class, complete assignments based on them, and have class discussions about them, remember that the basic purpose of a film is entertainment. Also, try to see how each film can teach you to interpret history and be a more critical viewer. Above all, enjoy the chance to evaluate and analyze a film "document" *actively* rather than being a passive receiver of its message.

Prehistory and the Origins of Civilization

— A Teacher's Guide to Feature Films and Documentary Sources —

Unfortunately, most world history courses must begin with the time period that is portrayed the most poorly in feature films. Because knowledge of prehistory and the earliest civilizations is mostly conjectural, films depicting these times tend to be ridiculous fantasies or even horror movies, such as *The Mummy's Curse.*

We do not recommend using a feature film for teaching about this time period. Rather, it is best to use one of the many documentaries covering these eras. They are often well-filmed on location and can provide more insights into prehistory and early history than can feature films. If you do choose to view feature films, an annotated list is given below. It is followed by a description of many useful documentaries, with comments about their length and availability.

FEATURE FILMS

Clan of the Cave Bear (1986, 100 minutes) Based on Jean M. Auel's bestseller, this film stars Daryl Hannah as a Cro-Magnon girl who is adopted by a group of Neanderthals. Rated **R**

The Egyptian (1954, 140 minutes) This film is based on the book of the same title by Mika Waltari; it tells a version of the Akhenaten (Ikhnaton) story.

The First Emperor of China (1995, 42 minutes) This IMAX movie is about the rule of Qin Shihuang.

Land of the Pharaohs (1955, 105 minutes, cowritten by William Faulkner) This is a soap opera-like story about pyramid building.

Old Testament, from Genesis Through Job (1994–1997) This carefully "mainstream" series from Turner Television Network includes six sections: *Abraham* (1995, 159 minutes), *Jacob* (1994, 120 minutes), *Joseph* (1995, 240 minutes), *Moses* (1996, 240 minutes), *Samson and Delilah* (1997, 200 minutes), and *David* (1997, 200 minutes).

Prince of Egypt (1998, 97 minutes) A Dreamworks animated feature, this tells the Moses story.

Quest for Fire (1981, 97 minutes) Directed by Jean-Jacques Annaud, this movie was filmed in Kenya, Scotland, Iceland, and Canada. It includes languages and gestures created especially for the characters by author Anthony Burgess and sociologist Desmond Morris. It may be a good representation of early human behavior but, unfortunately, it is rated **R** and may be inappropriate for schools.

The Ten Commandments (1956, 219 minutes) This Cecil B. De Mille biblical spectacle tells the story of Moses and the liberation of his people, the Israelites, from Egypt. The movie is well known for its pageantry, costumes, and sets, as well as for dramatic cinematic moments such as the parting of the Red Sea.

DOCUMENTARIES

The first two episodes of Basil Davidson's *Africa* television series, "Different But Equal" and "Mastering the Continent" (1986, 50 minutes each), provide an introduction to archaeology in Africa. The first two parts of Jacob Bronowski's PBS series, *The Ascent of Man,* deal with prehistory: "Lower Than Angels" and "Harvest of the Seasons." NOVA produced a series titled *In Search of Human Origins* (1994, 180 minutes), which deals with archaeology and its use in tracing human evolution. NOVA also produced *Ice Mummies* (1998, 180 minutes), which looks at how the preserved remains of humans can shed light on ancient cultures. The History Channel program *The Cavemen: In Search of History* (1997, 50 minutes) deals with Neanderthal humans. The BBC has produced a seven-part program narrated by Richard Leakey titled *The Making of Mankind* (1981, 55 minutes each); this is a comprehensive look at the "treasure hunt" for our human beginnings. One segment of Insight Media's *Africa Before the Europeans* series is "The Ancient Africans" (1970, 27 minutes); it traces African societies from the Stone Age to the age of European discovery. Another program in the same series, "Africa: Historical Heritage" (1985, 90 minutes) focuses on ancient Kush. A more recent five-part series from the same company explores *Lost Civilizations: Non-Western Cultures* (1995, 60 minutes each). The Learning Channel (TLC) has produced a 10-part documentary series entitled *Archaeology* (1994, 600 minutes). The five videos contain two programs each on *Primal Man, Mysteries of Egypt, Holy Land Revealed,* and *Secrets of the Aztecs and Maya.*

There is a wealth of documentary material on Egypt. In 1971 Sir Kenneth Clark presented a cultural survey, *Ancient Egypt* (51 minutes), which is available on video from Time/Life or UCAL Video. *The Mystery of Nefertiti* (1975, 45 minutes) and *Champollion: Egyptian Hieroglyphics* (1970, 33 minutes) are two productions that deal with archaeological work in uncovering Egypt's past. *Ancient Lives* is an eight-part series on film or video produced by Films for the Humanities (1985); it documents the lives of the craftsmen who built the tombs in the Valley of the Kings. Each program is approximately 28 minutes. A one-hour program that was part of the PBS Odyssey series deals with the deciphering of hieroglyphics, *The Key to the Land of Silence* (PBS Video). The History Channel has a 50-minute video titled *Secrets of the Rosetta Stone,* and A&E offers an overview of Egyptian writing simply titled *Hieroglyphics.* For middle-school students, United Learning has a 28-minute video with teacher materials, *Ancient Egypt: Gift of the Nile.* National Geographic offers two videos that provide good overviews of Egypt: *Egypt: Quest for Eternity* (60 minutes) and *Mysteries of Egypt* (1998, 90 minutes). David Macaulay's *Pyramid* (1988, 60 minutes), produced by PBS, uses animation to tell its story. *This Old Pyramid* (1992, 90 minutes), produced by NOVA, uses the *This Old House* approach to reconstruct a pyramid.

There are documentaries available on ancient civilizations other than Egypt. The series hosted by Abba Eban on PBS called *Heritage: Civilization and the Jews* is available on video from Films Inc. Each segment is 60 minutes; the first two episodes deal with the pre-Christian era. A&E has several documentaries on biblical history. A 13-part series exploring *Mysteries of the Bible* is available in a boxed set of six videocassettes (660 minutes total). There is also a two-part video set (140 minutes) titled *Who Wrote the Bible?* A&E has also packaged six episodes from the *Biography* series into an *Old Testament Collection* (350 minutes total). A 58-minute documentary called *The Royal Archives of Ebla* (1980) is distributed by Films Inc. The *Legacy* series from Maryland Public Television (1991, 57 minutes per episode) explores ancient Iraq, India, Egypt, China, and Central America, as well as the barbarian tribes in western Europe. The *Lost Treasures* series (2000, 50 minutes per segment) includes "Ancient China," "Ancient India," and "Samurai Japan." A program in NOVA's *Secrets of Lost Empires* series explores the mysteries of "Stonehenge" (1992, 60 minutes). The History Channel has two videos on ancient China: *Tomb of the Terra Cotta Warriors* (2000, 50 minutes) and *The Great Wall* (1997, 50 minutes).

TEACHER'S GUIDE

ULYSSES

Paramount Pictures, 1954; directed by Mario Camerini, color, 102 minutes

BACKGROUND OF THE FILM

This film was the result of an Italian-American collaboration. Seven writers worked on the screenplay, including Ben Hecht and Irwin Shaw. It is a simplified and fairly loose adaptation of the Greek epic poem *The Odyssey,* which tells the story of the adventures of Odysseus (Ulysses) on his journey home to the Greek island of Ithaca after fighting in the Trojan War.

Most feature films dealing with this time in history are either historical epics or performances of the Greek plays. This film falls into the first category. Out of the original long adventure story, the writers only chose random episodes and left out much for the sake of condensing the time. (Odysseus wandered for 10 years before returning to his native land.) The character of Ulysses is also flawed. In Homer's *Odyssey,* the hero trusts his wisdom rather than his strength; in the film, Ulysses is impetuous and foolhardy. Reviewers of this film have suggested that this character change might have been made to give Kirk Douglas, the actor who plays Ulysses, every opportunity to flex his muscles. One review even described this portrayal of Ulysses as a Villanova halfback on summer vacation in the Mediterranean (Robert Hatch, *Nation,* September 3, 1955).

Despite its flaws, any telling of the Ulysses story can be used in studying ancient Greece. All of the scholastic arguments about Homer and his existence aside, the importance of the Homeric epics is that they were like a bible to the Greeks. *The Iliad* and *The Odyssey* were the foundation of Greek education and an integral part of Greek cultural life. Their recitations were the chief form of entertainment and chief source of history for the Greeks, although the epics presented an idealized, legendary Heroic Age. The Greek gods are portrayed as capricious and amoral, a contrast to the supreme being of the Hebrews, who was a perfect moral example.

This movie was filmed on location in the Mediterranean, and the costumes were designed from Greek vase paintings with Homeric themes. Some of the dialogue is taken directly from *The Odyssey,* but much is modern invention. Be aware of the fact that the film was dubbed from Italian, and the lip synchronization is not always perfect. Kirk Douglas spoke his lines in English, was dubbed into Italian, and then redubbed back into English (a curious feature).

SYNOPSIS OF THE PLOT

The film opens with a scene of Ulysses' ship; a narrator describes the Trojan War and the anger of the god Neptune over the destruction of his temple.

The scene then switches to Ithaca, where Penelope, Ulysses' wife, has been waiting for his return from Troy. Believing that Ulysses is dead, parasitic suitors are living in her house and pressuring her to marry one of them. Meanwhile, Ulysses has washed up on a beach in the kingdom of Phaeacia and cannot remember who he is. He is taken in by the king, Alcinous, and proves his prowess as a wrestler in games held to honor the gods. The scene switches once more to Ithaca, where the dominant suitor, Antinous, forces Penelope to promise that she will choose one of the suitors on the day of the Games of Apollo.

In Phaeacia, Ulysses is preparing to marry the king's daughter, Nausicaa, when he begins to remember his ship and its near breakup in a storm.

A series of flashbacks recounts Ulysses' adventures with his crew: A landing party searches an island for food and supplies. Ulysses and his men get trapped in the cave of Polyphemus the Cyclops, son of Neptune. Ulysses uses trickery to blind Polyphemus and escape. As he departs the island, Ulysses boasts of his deed and his family descent. The ship is sailing toward Ithaca when the crew experiences a strange calm and odor. They are passing the rocks of the Sirens, whose songs lure men to their deaths. Ulysses has his men put wax in their ears, while he has himself lashed to the mast so that he can hear their songs. Next, the ship is drawn to the mysterious island controlled by Circe, the witch. Ulysses is bewitched by Circe and stays with her for six months. In desperation, his men set sail without him. The ship is caught in a storm and the men are drowned, while Ulysses helplessly watches from shore. Circe tempts Ulysses to stay by saying that she will make him a god. She conjures up Agamemnon, Achilles, and their men from the land of the dead, who bewail their fate. The unbidden appearance of his mother, who has died while waiting for Ulysses to return home, brings Ulysses to reality. He prepares to leave Circe and tries once more to reach Ithaca.

The flashback ends. Ulysses remembers who he is and begs King Alcinous for a boat so that he can reach home. Meanwhile, in Ithaca, the suitors are preparing for the Games of Apollo to win Penelope's hand. A beggar comes to visit Penelope with news of Ulysses. Unbeknownst to her, it is Ulysses in disguise. He tells her to hold a contest at the games to choose a husband. Penelope begins the contest, which is to bend the bow of Ulysses. One by one the suitors try and fail. The beggar steps forward; he easily strings and bends the bow. Ulysses reveals that he has

returned. In a rage, he destroys the suitors. Penelope and Ulysses are reunited, and Ulysses promises her many years of happiness.

IDEAS FOR CLASS DISCUSSION

The Iliad and The Odyssey were probably stories or poems told orally long before Homer wrote them down. They are characteristic of a period in Greek history known as the Dark Ages (ca. 1200–700 B.C.E.), when written language went out of use. It was a time of warfare. Powerful noble families proclaimed their descent from gods and heroes of the past. A good theme for class discussion is how this film typifies the time period. Also, the differences between the Greek gods and the god of the Hebrews is a good topic. The Greek gods do not have moral values; they are capricious and willful and do not show mercy to humans on the basis of their goodness. The god of the Hebrews is not only one god (showing monotheism) but has moral values and ethical attributes.

BOOKS AND MATERIALS
RELATING TO THIS FILM AND TOPIC

Coolidge, Olivia. *The Trojan War* (Houghton Mifflin, 1952).

Hamilton, Edith. *The Greek Way* (W. W. Norton, 1958).

Homer. *The Odyssey,* trans. Robert Fagles (Penguin, 1999).

Kitto, H.D.F. *The Greeks* (Penguin Books, 1951).

Wood, Michael. *In Search of the Trojan War* (BBC Books, 1985).

OTHER MEDIA RESOURCES
FOR THIS TIME PERIOD

Alexander the Great (1956, 135 minutes) Richard Burton plays the title role in this film, which is historically accurate.

Helen of Troy (Italian, 1955, 118 minutes) This Robert Wise film of the Trojan War is rather lackluster.

The Odyssey (1997, 173 minutes) Based on a Hallmark Hall of Fame television miniseries, this is a condensed version of the original 240-minute series with vivid special effects.

Socrates (1979, 120 minutes) Directed by Roberto Rossellini, this film is carefully researched and well presented; in Italian with English subtitles.

The Trojan Horse (1962, 105 minutes) Based on *The Iliad,* this Italian film deals with the Homeric Age and the Trojan War; dubbed in English.

There are also many movies made of the Greek plays that, although difficult, can add to an understanding of Greek attitudes and philosophy.

Antigone (1962, 88 minutes) This is the third play of the Oedipus cycle.

Medea (1971, 100 minutes) This film features Maria Callas in her first acting role; in Italian with English subtitles.

Oedipus the King (1967, 97 minutes) This film stars Orson Welles and Christopher Plummer. It was filmed in a Greek amphitheater using modern English idiom.

Oedipus Tyrannus (1978, 60 minutes) This BBC version begins when Oedipus discovers his father's death.

The Trojan Women (1971, 105 minutes) This Euripides play has an all-star cast featuring Katharine Hepburn, Vanessa Redgrave, Irene Pappas, and Genevieve Bujold.

Ancient Greece

ULYSSES

Paramount Pictures, 1954, directed by Mario Camerini.

Major Character	Actor/Actress
Ulysses	Kirk Douglas
Penelope/Circe	Silvana Mangano
Telemachus	Franco Interlenghi
Antinous	Anthony Quinn
Nausicaa	Rosanna Podesta
Euriclea	Sylvie
Euroloco	Daniel Ivernei
Alcinous	Jacque Dumesnil

WHAT TO WATCH FOR

This film is an adaptation of *The Odyssey,* a Greek epic poem. It is generally credited to Homer, but the poem actually had its origins as an oral story years earlier. It tells the story of a Greek hero, Odysseus (or Ulysses), who has fought in the Trojan War. He then travels for 10 years trying to reach Ithaca, his home in Greece. The actual poem contains many adventures. The film selects three: the adventure with Polyphemus, the Cyclops; the lure of the Sirens; and the meeting with Circe, the witch.

Notice the ship of Ulysses and his crew; it is typical of Greek vessels of the Homeric and Classic ages. The costumes also are historically accurate, based on paintings on Greek vases. Notice, too, the Greek emphasis on omen and prophecy. This is a common theme running through Greek literature. The storyteller who sets the scene in the beginning is a typical feature of many early civilizations. Homer may have learned the poem from a storyteller whose tales were later set down in writing.

(continued)

The movie portrays the Greek love of games—really athletic competitions held to honor the gods. Wrestling was very popular, with no holds barred. Competitions were a way of proving one's heroic nature. The hero was important to the ancient Greeks as an embodiment of human ideals.

This film gives us a view of the Greek gods. They are pictured as capricious and vengeful. "The gods are playful and without mercy," Ulysses shouts as the Sirens sing their mysterious songs. The tragedies that befall Ulysses are a result of his defiance of the gods—particularly Neptune. This is a common theme in Greek plays. Despite his trials, through his cleverness and strength, Ulysses is able to return home. He defeats his rivals and is reunited with his wife, Penelope, and his son, Telemachus.

Screening Notes

Ancient Greece

— *ULYSSES* —

VOCABULARY

Cyclops   Neptune
Homeric Age   Siren
hubris   Troy

QUESTIONS BASED ON THE FILM

1. Why does Cassandra place a curse upon Ulysses?

   _____

   _____

   _____

2. Weaving was an important occupation for Greek women. How does Penelope use weaving to keep her independence?

   _____

   _____

   _____

3. How does Ulysses escape from the Cyclops?

   _____

   _____

   _____

(continued)

4. Why do the Sirens sing their songs? How do Ulysses and his men deal with their enchantment?

_____

_____

_____

5. How does Circe tempt Ulysses to stay with her? Why does he change his mind?

_____

_____

_____

6. Give examples from the movie that demonstrate the nature of the Greek gods. How do they differ from the deity of the Hebrews?

_____

_____

_____

_____

7. What attributes of a hero does Ulysses demonstrate? What are his strengths? What are his weaknesses?

_____

_____

_____

_____

TEACHER'S GUIDE

A FUNNY THING HAPPENED ON THE WAY TO THE FORUM

United Artists, 1966; directed by Richard Lester, color, 99 minutes

BACKGROUND OF THE FILM

A Funny Thing Happened on the Way to the Forum is based on the plays of the Roman playwright Titus Maccius Plautus. Plautus was born about 254 B.C.E. in Umbria, a region of north central Italy. It appears that he moved to Rome at an early age to earn his livelihood by all kinds of theatrical work. Over 130 plays are attributed to Plautus. Like many playwrights of his time, Plautus often took amusing Greek plays and rewrote them to entertain Roman audiences. *A Funny Thing* is a pastiche of scenes from many of Plautus' plays. A strong element is farce, a light, humorous type of drama that allows great latitude in portraying the probability of happenings and the naturalness of characters. Farce has a strong element of repressed fantasy. Plautus used this comedy, often performed at breakneck speed, to satirize sex, the family, marriage, money, social caste, and many other elements of Roman society.

Drama in Plautus' time was far different from the sophisticated Greek theater, where the plays themselves were the focus of major festivals. Rome had four annual festivals, during which many special events were held (such as victory celebrations) and dramas were presented. Dramas were only part of these programs, which also included gladiators, wrestlers, and tightrope walkers. The crowds were motley and often rude. The playwright *had* to amuse. Plautus

knew how to write for a popular audience, and he became famous and successful.

Plautus was also history's first known writer of what we today call musical comedy. The songs interjected throughout *A Funny Thing* are typical of Plautus' style, although we do not have copies of the melodies that Plautus used, only the words. Slapstick, the use of puns, clowning, gesticulation, and comic alliteration are all characteristic of Plautine drama. Plautus used type characters, or stock characters, again and again: Pseudolus, the crafty, scheming slave; Miles, the bragging, bullying soldier; the young Hero who seeks to wed one forbidden to him; the lecherous Lycus, a professional procurer of women.

Director Richard Lester has used quick cuts, rapid movement of scenes, and the juxtaposition of absurd images to give us a sense of farce in a broad Roman comedy. However, he has also infused the musical with the burlesque typical of the late 1950s and early 1960s before the women's liberation movement. The women in *A Funny Thing* are predominantly sex objects to be tempted by and bargained for.

The movie is useful for two major reasons. It is, with the reservations stated above, a good example of a Roman comedy in the tradition of Plautus. The film is also useful for atmosphere, something that director Lester is particularly good at. The costumes and the settings show us a Roman neighborhood, not the glorified Forum or massive public buildings. The street scenes with marching soldiers, merchants peddling their wares, and slaves being bought and sold give us a flavor of the crowded, bustling activity of Rome, one of the world's first great urban centers.

SYNOPSIS OF THE PLOT

Taken from several of Plautus' plays, the plot is convoluted and really inconsequential; it is the joking and jesting that are important.

The film opens in a Roman marketplace with the main character, Pseudolus the slave. He introduces the story and characters by singing "Comedy Tonight." Pseudolus is obsessed with trying to win his freedom from his master, Senex, and mistress, Domina. The master and mistress leave their home. Their son, Hero, is in the safekeeping of Hysterium, their slave of slaves. They have warned Hysterium not to let Hero near the house next door. It is owned by Marcus Lycus, a procurer dealing in beautiful courtesans.

Hero is in love with a girl named Philia in the house of ill repute. Pseudolus promises to procure her if Hero will give him his freedom. Philia has already been sold, but Pseudolus tricks Lycus into giving her to Hero. Hysterium breaks up the happy couple, but Pseudolus blackmails him to allow Hero and Philia an hour together.

Philia feels bound by her original contract to her purchaser, a captain in the army. Hero and Pseudolus go off to concoct a potion to make her change her mind. Senex suddenly returns home and finds Philia. Pseudolus, thinking quickly, says that she is the new maid. To get Senex out of the way, Pseudolus and Hysterium send him next door to a house vacated by Erronious, an old man who has been searching for his long-lost children. Senex goes into the house to take a bath, when Erronius suddenly appears. Hysterium and Pseudolus stop him at the door and tell him that his house is haunted. Pseudolus masquerades as a soothsayer. He sends Erronius off to run up the hills of Rome to break the curse.

Meanwhile, emissaries from the captain arrive at Lycus's house and demand Philia. Lycus convinces Pseudolus to trade places with him, which Pseudolus does gladly, since he has fallen in love with one of the courtesans. The courtesans are sent to Senex's house for safekeeping while the captain, Miles Gloriosus, rides to claim his bride. In the midst of this, Domina returns. Pseudolus saves the situation by telling her that she is lucky to be entertaining a great Roman captain.

Miles threatens Pseudolus with death in two minutes if his bride is not delivered. Philia refuses to go to the captain; she now recognizes him as the destroyer of her homeland. Pseudolus dresses Hysterium as a bride and brings him in on a bier, saying that the virgin has died. The captain decides that his bride should be cremated. Hero, looking upon the scene, thinks that Philia has died. He pledges to throw himself to the lions. Philia is told that Hero is gone; she pledges to offer herself as a sacrifice.

Hysterium and Pseudolus escape to prevent the young lovers' suicides. Pseudolus enters the gladiator school and saves Hero from death. Hero then rushes to save Philia. A wild chariot scene ensues, with almost all of the major characters involved.

The captain captures the conspirators, and everyone is brought back to Rome for execution. A happy ending is ensured when Erronious appears and the captain and Philia are proved to be his long-lost children. Hero and Philia are betrothed, Pseudolus gets his freedom, and the entire cast reprises "Comedy Tonight."

IDEAS FOR CLASS DISCUSSION

Three major threads for class discussion could be slavery in the Roman Empire, urban conditions, and entertainment. Slavery was a fact of life in the ancient world. An interesting topic for discussion could be how ancient slavery differed from slavery in the United States, where the opportunity to buy one's freedom was rare and there were racial differences between slaves and their owners. Rome was very much an urban empire, with many of the problems we associate with twenty-first-century cities: overcrowding, traffic, shortage of housing, and deterioration of the infrastructure. How are these problems like conditions today? How are they different? Entertainment in the Roman Empire was designed for the masses; it offered a way to keep people placated. Modern television programing has been described as mind candy. Are we any more sophisticated than the Romans?

BOOKS AND MATERIALS RELATING TO THIS FILM AND TOPIC

Casson, Lionel, ed. *Masters of Ancient Comedy* (Macmillan, 1960).

Corrigan, Robert W., ed. *Roman Drama* (Dell Publishing, 1966).

Durant, Will. *Caesar and Christ* (Simon & Schuster, 1944).

Grant, Michael. *The World of Rome* (World Publishing, 1960).

Johnston, Mary. *Roman Life* (Scott Foresman, 1957).

Norwood, Gilbert. *Plautus and Terence* (Cooper Square Publishers, 1963).

OTHER MEDIA RESOURCES FOR THIS TIME PERIOD

Gladiator (2000, 155 minutes) This Academy Award-winning film is about a fictitious Roman general who is discredited by a rival and must fight his way to freedom. Not that Ancient Rome wasn't violent, but this is too violent for classroom use. Rated **R**

Hannibal (1960, 103 minutes) This film has authentic-looking sets, but the performances are rather wooden; dubbed from Italian.

I, Claudius (1976, 13 parts, 840 minutes total) This PBS series is based on Robert Graves's book of the same name. It covers the period from the emperor Augustus to the emperor Claudius.

Julius Caesar (1953, 121 minutes) This is probably the best production of Shakespeare's play, with Marlon Brando playing Mark Antony.

The Romans: Life, Laughter, and Law (1971, 27 minutes) This is part of Learning Corporation of America's *Western Civilization: Majesty and Madness* series. Although not a feature-length film, *The Romans* contains performances of Roman literature and plays, including an excerpt from Plautus's *The Braggart Soldier*. It is a highly entertaining overview of Roman philosophy and life.

Spartacus (1960, 192 minutes) Directed by Stanley Kubrick and based on a novel by Howard Fast, this film centers on the abortive slave uprising of 73 B.C.E. It offers an excellent view of issues of oppression and resistance. New versions of this classic restore the 12 minutes cut from the original.

Ancient Rome

—————— *A Funny Thing Happened on the Way to the Forum* ——————

United Artists, 1966; directed by Richard Lester

Major Character	Actor/Actress
Pseudolus	Zero Mostel
Marcus Lycus	Phil Silvers
Erronius	Buster Keaton
Hysterium	Jack Gilford
Senex	Michael Hordern
Domina	Patricia Jessel
Hero	Michael Crawford
Philia	Annette Andre
Miles Gloriosus	Leon Greene

WHAT TO WATCH FOR

This film is based on the plays of the Roman comic playwright Plautus (ca. 254–184 B.C.E.). Plautus adapted Greek drama to Roman conditions. He wrote for a popular and, at times, even crude audience. Plautus made use of slapstick, burlesque, sight gags, and puns to amuse his audience. He also used stock characters who would be familiar to Romans of his day. This film treatment, with its broad comedy and rapid cuts, is true to the style of Plautus. Watch for the use of the quick comic line and the unsophisticated nature of the humor.

The film, besides giving us a taste of Roman drama, also conveys the atmosphere of ancient Rome. The action takes place in a Roman neighborhood, not around the public buildings of the Forum. Notice the street scenes, the activities, and the costumes. Notice also the architecture of the buildings: The house interiors are those of fairly wealthy Romans.

(continued)

Slavery was an important Roman institution. It began during the early Republic with prisoners of war. Upon capture, they forfeited their freedom instead of their lives. They were then sold by wholesale slave dealers. Later, in the time of the Empire, Rome became the greatest slave market in the world. Slaves were brought in from many sources—some from warfare, some from professional slave hunters, and others from the breeding of slaves. This type of slavery is very different from the pre-Civil War slavery in the United States, where slavery was mainly confined to a specific race. Also, while Roman slaves, as in the American South, could be field hands, many were well educated and highly skilled. A Greek slave could be highly prized as a *paedagogus,* or tutor, to the children of a well-to-do Roman. Every wealthy Roman family had a number of personal slaves. They served family members as maids or butlers, hairdressers or barbers, or did household chores. Slaves were able to buy their freedom. Like Pseudolus, they could also receive freedom as a reward for a special act of devotion. The master only had to declare, before witnesses, that the slave was free.

Screening Notes

Ancient Rome

A FUNNY THING HAPPENED ON THE WAY TO THE FORUM

VOCABULARY

aqueduct   Jupiter

farce   legion satire

Forum   soothsayer

gladiator   vestal virgins

QUESTIONS BASED ON THE FILM

1. Describe a typical Roman city street. What are some of the activities that might go on there?

   _____

   _____

   _____

   _____

2. Describe the ways in which Roman slavery was different from slavery in the American South. Give specific examples from the film.

   _____

   _____

   _____

   _____

(continued)

3. The Romans were used to the presence of soldiers in their cities and towns. Plautus often satirized soldiers in his drama. How does the film show this?

_____

_____

_____

_____

4. How is Roman comedy like ours? How is it different? Can you think of any comedians, movies, or television shows that use the devices of Roman comedy?

_____

_____

_____

_____

The Middle Ages

TEACHER'S GUIDE

THE LION IN WINTER

Avco Embassy Pictures, 1968; directed by Anthony Harvey, color, 135 minutes; nominated for seven Academy Awards. Katharine Hepburn won an Oscar® for Best Actress; the film also received an Oscar for Best Musical Score.

BACKGROUND OF THE FILM

This film is based on a play of the same name by James Goldman. The historical figures in the movie and play did exist, but the event portrayed is fictitious. Eleanor of Aquitaine (1122–1204) was one of the dominant figures of the twelfth century. The heiress of the rich lands of Aquitaine and Poitou in France, she was married to King Louis Capet when she was 15, bringing her lands as a dowry. Since Eleanor did not produce a male heir, Louis divorced her on the grounds of consanguinity (blood relationship). At the age of 30, she was married to 18-year-old Henry Plantagenet, who gathered her lands into his possession and became King Henry II of England in 1154. Eleanor gave birth to five sons while married to Henry, but she sought to control her four surviving sons and her lands as she saw fit, even setting up her own court in Poitiers, France.

Henry declared his eldest son, Henry, as his successor, but Eleanor's favorite son, Richard (known as the Lion-Hearted) was declared the inheritor of Aquitaine and Poitou. Geoffrey was given Brittany, and John, the youngest, got nothing. The three older sons rose in rebellion against their father to gain more land and prestige; Eleanor was regarded as the instigator. Henry placed Eleanor in captivity for 15 years, only letting her out from time to time to attend an Easter or Christmas court. *The Lion in Winter* tells of a fictional family reunion at a Christmas court held at Chinon Castle in 1183. The young heir to the throne, Henry, has died the previous June; thus a family conference is necessary to deal with the problem of succession.

Although family conferences were held, what actually happened in this case is not known. James Goldman has turned the occasion of a Christmas court into a drama of personality and relationships. The characters are portrayed as contemporary figures in medieval dress. Modern psychology is used to explain how historical figures might have behaved.

Great pains were taken by the production crew to find genuine twelfth-century buildings to act as settings. Since little of Chinon Castle remained, other twelfth-century structures in France were used, such as Montmajour Abbey for interiors, Chateau de Roy Rena for exterior shots, and the walled city of Carcassonne for other exterior footage. Other scenes were shot at Ardmore studios in Dublin, where castle interiors were reconstructed. Research was done to ensure that the costumes and interior decor were as authentic as possible and that the somewhat primitive living conditions of the time were accurately portrayed. Note the scene in which King Henry must break a sheet of ice in a water basin in order to wash his face. The scene in the dungeon was filmed in the vault of Montmajour Abbey; it took eight days to shoot in unpleasant conditions of dampness, mice, and foul air.

SYNOPSIS OF THE PLOT

It is Christmas 1183. The heir to the English throne has been dead for six months. Henry II summons his three remaining sons; his estranged wife, Eleanor of Aquitaine; and King Philip II of France to a conference regarding succession to the throne. Henry favors his youngest son, John, while Richard is Eleanor's choice. Also at the conference is Philip's sister, Princess Alais, who has been promised as a wife to the heir to the throne. Alais has been brought up in Henry's court to fulfill this vow and has a rich dowry, a region called the Vexin. To complicate matters, Alais has become Henry's mistress, and he is loath to give her up.

To appease Eleanor, Henry announces that Alais and the crown will go to Richard. This does not fool Eleanor, who knows that the promise is a ruse and that Henry wants John to succeed him. Eleanor demands an immediate marriage between Richard and Alais and promises Aquitaine to Henry if he concurs. The wedding ceremony is broken up when Richard learns of the deal and threatens war with Henry. Eleanor sends Richard to Philip to form an alliance, but the young king of France plays politics as well. He exposes Richard as a homosexual (historical documents reveal that Richard and Philip had shared a bed when Richard visited Paris) and Geoffrey and John as traitors. Henry disowns his sons. He orders them locked in the dungeon of Chinon. Henry tells Eleanor that he will seek an annulment of their marriage, marry Alais, and produce a new heir to the throne. Alais refuses to marry Henry unless he rids himself of his sons to prevent them from murdering any child she might have. Henry goes to the dungeon, but finds Eleanor and his sons armed and plotting his death. Getting the upper hand, Henry prepares to kill Richard but cannot do so. When Eleanor invites him to try to kill her, he also falters.

The Christmas court dissolves with few issues settled. The sons and Philip leave the castle. Henry and Eleanor part as affectionate adversaries who realize that their lives are irrevocably entwined.

IDEAS FOR CLASS DISCUSSION

This film owes a huge part of its dialogue to the interest in "pop psychology" that arose in the 1960s. Some critics jokingly called this film *Who's Afraid of Eleanor of Acquitaine?* after the psychological drama *Who's Afraid of Virginia Woolf?* A good topic for discussion might be how this plays out in the dialogue and action of this film. How can we possibly know how medieval people thought and what they talked about in their private moments? The conditions of medieval life should also be noted. So many fantasy stories and animated films romanticize the Middle Ages that a good topic for discussion would be the actual primitive conditions of sanitation and housing. An important aspect of this film is the emphasis on who will inherit the throne. England had gone through a civil war over the issue of legitimate claim to the monarchy. Henry's ascension to the throne was the result of a "deal" made by the warring parties. Henry was more than aware that a strong, clear line of descent and dynastic claim to the throne was essential for the peace and security of the realm.

BOOKS AND MATERIALS RELATING TO THIS FILM AND TOPIC

Dickens, Homer. *The Films of Katharine Hepburn* (The Citadel Press, 1971).

Goldman, James. *The Lion in Winter* (Penguin Books, 1983).

Hallam, Elizabeth. *Plantagenet Chronicles, Vol. I* (Weidenfield, 1986).

Kelly, Amy. *Eleanor of Aquitaine and the Four Kings* (Harvard University Press, 1950).

Seward, Desmond. *Eleanor of Aquitaine, Mother Queen* (Dorset Press, 1978).

OTHER MEDIA RESOURCES FOR THIS TIME PERIOD

The Adventures of Robin Hood (1938, 102 minutes) This is a real adventure film, with Errol Flynn as the swashbuckling hero.

Becket (1964, 148 minutes) The story takes place at an earlier time than *The Lion in Winter,* with Peter O'Toole again playing King Henry II. The plot deals with Henry's stormy relationship with his archbishop, Thomas Becket (Richard Burton).

Brother Sun, Sister Moon (1972, 121 minutes) This is Franco Zeffirelli's film about St. Francis of Assisi.

El Cid (1961, 184 minutes) This story of Rodrigo Diaz and his battle to free Spain from Muslim rule is somewhat simplified; El Cid actually fought for both the Christians and the Muslims, depending on the stakes offered.

The Warlord (1965, 121 minutes) Charlton Heston stars as an eleventh-century Norman knight who is warlord over a village and falls in love with one of the peasant girls.

The Middle Ages

THE LION IN WINTER

Avco Embassy Pictures, 1968; directed by Anthony Harvey

Major Character	Actor/Actress
Henry II	Peter O'Toole
Eleanor of Aquitaine	Katharine Hepburn
Princess Alais	Jane Merrow
Prince Geoffrey	John Castle
Prince Richard (the Lion-Hearted)	Anthony Hopkins
John	Nigel Terry
Philip of France	Timothy Dalton
Marshall	Nigel Stock

WHAT TO WATCH FOR

This film is about a family conference in 1183. It is called by King Henry II to decide who will be his successor as king of England. Although such conferences did take place, we do not know precisely what took place at them. The author, James Goldman, has turned a fictitious conference into a setting for a complex personal drama. Modern psychology has been used to interpret what might have happened.

Be aware of the complicated nature of feudal holdings. Eleanor had been married earlier to King Louis VII of France, who wanted her dowry (the rich lands of Aquitaine and Poitou). When she did not produce a male heir, Louis divorced Eleanor on the grounds that they were blood relatives. Eleanor was then married to Henry Plantagenet, who became King Henry II of England. It is important to remember that the king of England was also the duke of Normandy, and therefore a vassal of the French king. The ambition of the English kings to gain more French lands, and the desire of the French kings to prevent this, was a major theme for many years of the Middle Ages. Marriages were a good way to gain valuable

(continued)

territory. For example, with Princess Alais, sister of the king of France, came her dowry of a province called the Vexin, a land Henry desired for its strategic location.

Note how the film portrays living conditions in the Middle Ages. Castles have been much romanticized, but they were really damp, cold, and primitive. In the film, dogs freely wander through the halls, reminding us that hunting was an important medieval pastime.

Note also how the main historical characters are portrayed. Although the records are few, we do know that Henry was a strong king. He was concerned with making *his* law the common law of the land, instead of the fragmented feudal laws of each manor. Eleanor is considered one of the most powerful women in history. Richard did become king (1189–1199), but he was noted more for his skill as a warrior than as a ruler. John became king after Richard (1199–1216); his rule was disastrous for the English monarchy. He lost almost all of the English possessions in France. He also was forced by his nobles in 1215 to sign the Magna Carta, which limited the monarch's power.

Screening Notes

The Middle Ages

THE LION IN WINTER

VOCABULARY

annulment

court

crusade

dowry

dungeon

joust

Plantagenet dynasty

vassal

QUESTIONS BASED ON THE FILM

1. Marriage was an important political tool in the Middle Ages. Why has Henry married Eleanor? Why is he anxious to keep Alais?

_____

_____

_____

_____

_____

2. What is the courtyard of the castle like? How does this reflect the self-sufficient role of a castle?

_____

_____

_____

_____

_____

(continued)

3. Why does Henry keep Eleanor imprisoned in Salisbury Tower?

_____

_____

_____

_____

4. Eleanor states, "We are the origins of war, not history's forces, nor the times, nor justice, nor the lack of it, nor causes, nor religions, nor ideas, nor kinds of government." How is this true? How does this statement demonstrate the politics of feudalism?

_____

_____

_____

_____

5. Philip II of France became known as Augustus. What traits does he display in the film that might merit this title?

_____

_____

_____

6. Why is Henry so obsessed with planning for his succession? Can you think of other times in history when a fight over succession brought either dramatic changes or disastrous events?

_____

_____

_____

_____

_____

TEACHER'S GUIDE

THE AGONY AND THE ECSTASY

Twentieth Century-Fox, 1965; directed by Carol Reed, color, 139 minutes

BACKGROUND OF THE FILM

This film is based on the best-selling biographical novel about Michelangelo by Irving Stone. The studio invested $12 million in the production, which was not a financial success at the box office. Over 60 technicians were hired to recreate the Sistine Chapel ceiling at the de Laurentiis studio in Rome, where a full-scale set was constructed.

The plot revolves around one episode in Michelangelo's long (1475–1564) life: the painting of the fresco on the Sistine Chapel ceiling from 1508 to 1512. It also involves the artist's somewhat stormy relationship with Pope Julius II. Many events are historically accurate, such as the animosity between Michelangelo and the architect Bramante, the destruction of the first frescoes by Michelangelo and his decision to work alone, and the highly charged political situation in Italy (with the pope involved in many wars). However, certain liberties are taken with fact. Although, according to witnesses, Pope Julius did hit Michelangelo with a stick, the pope apologized and sent an emissary with a money gift. Michelangelo was, in fact, paid for his work; he did not suffer the kind of financial indignities shown in the film. The filmmakers added romantic interest in the figure of Contessina de Medici, which is unverified by historical accounts.

The film can be used as a teaching device in a number of ways, but two major themes stand out: the actual production of the Sistine Chapel fresco, and the role of Pope Julius II in European politics and the revolt against the Catholic Church beginning in 1517.

The film does show the process of fresco, the technique of painting on wet plaster, which was employed by Michelangelo on the ceiling. The artist and his assistants are shown transferring the line drawings (or cartoons) onto the fresh, damp plaster, the *intonaco*. Water-soluble pigments are then painted on the plaster and, as it dries, the pigments are bonded in. Further touches are then put on *a secco* (on the dry plaster). This 1965 movie shows the colors used by Michelangelo as pure and rich. Interestingly, a 1980s restoration of the 8,070-square-foot ceiling cleaned away several layers of glue and dirt. The result has demonstrated that Michelangelo was a master of color and that the ceiling was originally much more glowing and colorful than previously imagined.

Julius II (pope from 1503 to 1513) was one of the most powerful popes of the Renaissance. In many ways, he was typical of the papacy at that time. Deemed a better warrior than religious leader, he spent much of his time fighting either to keep or to expand his Papal States. The film does present views of the church-versus-state conflict experienced by medieval and Renaissance Europe. The scene between Julius and the emissary of the French king is interesting. It is worthwhile to point out to students that sponsoring art projects and fighting wars were expensive. Julius raised money by selling ecclesiastical offices throughout northern Europe and ordering the Dominicans to sell indulgences, particularly in Germany. These abuses are seen as contributing greatly to the spirit of protest and reform that ultimately led to the Protestant Reformation.

SYNOPSIS OF THE PLOT

The film opens with an aerial view of St. Peter's Basilica in Rome. There follows a narrated documentary surveying Michelangelo's work.

As the film proper begins, the credits are run over a scene that re-creates the quarrying of marble in the early sixteenth century. As oxen pull the marble block down the mountain from the quarry, two armies cross the path and engage in battle as the quarry drivers run and hide. The leader of the victorious army is revealed to be the pope, Julius II.

The scene switches to Rome. The marble is finally delivered to Michelangelo, who is working on the pope's tomb. The pope rides into the city amid great pomp and pageantry, as his escort throws coins to the people. Later, in Julius' council chamber, the pope reprimands the French emissary. Julius states that he is at war and must reclaim the Papal States. Michelangelo enters. Julius tells him to stop work on his tomb; it is taking too much time and money. The pope takes Michelangelo into the chapel built by Julius' uncle, Sixtus. Julius tells Michelangelo that the artist will have the honor of decorating the ceiling of the Sistine Chapel. Michelangelo exclaims that he is a sculptor, not a painter, and runs away to Florence. In Florence, he seeks out Giovanni de Medici, whom he tells that he has applied to become an architect to the sultan of Turkey. Giovanni warns Michelangelo that if he should go to Turkey, he must stay there as long as Julius is pope. Michelangelo and his old friend, Contessina de Medici, talk of the pope's commission. Michelangelo does return to Rome with some Florentine assistants to begin work on the Sistine Chapel frescoes. He builds a scaffolding superior to one constructed by the architect Bramante and begins to trace the gigantic designs.

Michelangelo is uninspired by his work. He takes solace in a local tavern, where he studies the faces of people for his sketches. In a rage, he returns to the chapel and destroys his first designs. Julius hears of this while preparing to go to war. He orders that Michelangelo be sought out and brought before him.

Soldiers search throughout Italy for Michelangelo. The artist has gone up into the quarries in the mountains. Escaping even farther into the mountains, Michelangelo has a vision that inspires him with an idea for the ceiling fresco. The pope's forces are besieging a town when Michelangelo is brought to Julius with the new designs for the chapel ceiling. The pope accepts the plan, and Michelangelo returns to Rome to begin the work.

Michelangelo labors on his back on the scaffolding while Julius continually shouts from below, "When will you make an end?" Michelangelo works so long and hard to complete the fresco that he damages his eyesight and falls ill. Contessina de Medici nurses him back to health. Bramante shows Julius Raphael's work and tries to convince the pope to replace the ailing Michelangelo. The pope visits Michelangelo's house and tells the artist that he has been freed from this commission; Raphael will finish the ceiling. This is, in reality, a ploy to get Michelangelo back to work as fast as possible. Michelangelo does return to complete the frescoes.

Julius receives word that his enemies are at the gates of Rome. He must prepare for war. Julius orders that the scaffolding be taken down even though Michelangelo's work is unfinished. Julius and Michelangelo argue violently. The pope declares that the commission is at an end. As Michelangelo packs, Raphael comes to see him to express his admiration and coax Michelangelo to go to the pope and apologize.

Julius is wounded in battle. Michelangelo visits him in his headquarters to ask for permission to finish the frescoes. Julius gives permission, but he warns the artist that it may be in vain; the pope's enemies will enter Rome and destroy all monuments to Julius.

Julius and his battered army return to Rome in defeat. Despite his wounds, Julius climbs the scaffolding to look at the fresco. The pope faints. While he makes his last confession, his allies finally come to his defense. Michelangelo visits Julius at his bedside and goads him into recovery. Rome is saved. A service of thanksgiving is held in the Sistine Chapel to commemorate the pope's recovery, his victory, and the completed ceiling.

IDEAS FOR CLASS DISCUSSION

This film would lend itself well to a discussion of the confused nature of politics during the Renaissance, when the pope was a secular as well as a religious leader. It was this kind of chaos that inspired Niccolò Machiavelli to write *The Prince*. In this treatise he outlines his theories on the importance of political power and how to achieve it. Another topic for class discussion might be the role of the artist in Renaissance society. The powerful families of that era felt a need to glorify their family name and demonstrate their prestige by hiring artists to produce works of art, very often to be prominently displayed in public locations. Do artists have the same kind of role today? Another worthwhile discussion might be about how artwork and the value placed on individual creative genius changed between the Middle Ages and the Renaissance.

BOOKS AND MATERIALS
RELATING TO THIS FILM AND TOPIC

Hale, John R., and the editors of Time-Life Books. *Renaissance* (Time-Life Books, 1965).

Lucas, Henry S. *The Renaissance and the Reformation* (Harper & Row, 1960).

Stone, Irving. *The Agony and the Ecstasy* (Doubleday, 1961).

Stone, Irving. *The Great Adventure of Michelangelo* (an abridged edition of *The Agony and the Ecstasy*) (Doubleday, 1961).

Vasari, Giorgio. *Lives of the Artists,* trans. George Bull (Penguin, 1966).

OTHER MEDIA RESOURCES
FOR THIS TIME PERIOD

The Age of the Medicis (1973, three episodes, 83 minutes each) This factual portrayal of the Italian Renaissance is presented by Roberto Rossellini in a three-part series made for Italian television.

Prince of Foxes (1949, 107 minutes) The subject of this film involves the intricate politics of Renaissance Italy. Orson Welles plays Cesare Borgia.

Romeo and Juliet (1968, 138 minutes) Franco Zeffirelli's version of the Shakespeare play includes beautiful settings and costuming.

The Renaissance

THE AGONY AND THE ECSTASY

Twentieth Century-Fox, 1965; directed by Carol Reed

Major Character	Actor/Actress
Michelangelo	Charlton Heston
Pope Julius II	Rex Harrison
Contessina de Medici	Diane Cilento
Bramante	Harry Andrews
Raphael	Tomas Milian
Duke of Urbino	Alberto Lupo
Giovanni de Medici	Adolfo Celi

WHAT TO WATCH FOR

This film was based on the biographical novel *The Agony and the Ecstasy* by Irving Stone. It was an expensive film to produce, costing $12 million and requiring over 60 technicians to re-create the huge frescoes found on the Sistine Chapel ceiling.

The movie accurately portrays how Michelangelo worked on the ceiling. Fresco is the process of painting on damp, freshly laid plaster so that the paint is bonded to the wall. For many years, it was felt that Michelangelo used muted colors for his design. A recent cleaning and restoration project has shown the colors to be bright and rich. The film shows the fresco colors as they have been revealed recently—an interesting fact, since the film was made 20 years before the restoration project.

Note the scene between Michelangelo and Raphael when they discuss the role of the artist and his patron. The necessity of patronage and securing commissions from wealthy clients began during this era. It has continued to plague artists, to a certain extent, up to the present.

(continued)

The film also accurately portrays the intricate and often violent politics of Renaissance Italy. Pope Julius was often considered a better warrior than religious leader. The movie shows the pope's role as secular leader of the Papal States as well as head of the Christian Church in Western Europe. In the film, one of the cardinals justifies Julius's role as a warrior. He says that the pope must fight his secular enemies to maintain an independent Church free from the control of European princes. This is, and has been, a subject for debate. When you view and discuss this film, keep in mind the role of the papacy in medieval and Renaissance Europe. Also consider the growing protests during that time against the political and economic ambitions of the popes.

Screening Notes

The Renaissance

THE AGONY AND THE ECSTASY

VOCABULARY

Bramante

cardinal

de Medici family

fresco

papacy

Papal States

Raphael

St. Peter's Basilica

secular

QUESTIONS BASED ON THE FILM

1. What was the political situation in Italy during the Renaissance? How is this shown in the film?

_____

_____

_____

_____

2. Historically, why did popes fear the French king?

_____

_____

_____

(continued)

3. In the film, Michelangelo has an argument with two cardinals who criticize his work. How do these cardinals represent, to a certain extent, the medieval view of art, as well as the view of some Renaissance scholars?

_____

_____

_____

4. How were artists in the Renaissance restricted by their need for a patron and funding?

_____

_____

_____

5. How did Julius raise money? How did this affect the declining prestige of the papacy?

_____

_____

_____

_____

6. How is Julius's role as warrior justified by his cardinals?

_____

_____

_____

_____

TEACHER'S GUIDE

A MAN FOR ALL SEASONS

Columbia Pictures Corporation, 1966; directed by Fred Zinnemann, color, 120 minutes. This film won three Academy Awards: Best Picture, Best Actor (Paul Scofield), and Best Director of 1966.

BACKGROUND OF THE FILM

Sir Thomas More was born in 1478. He was a lawyer, a scholar of international reputation, and the author of the book *Utopia*. More became a judge in King Henry VIII's court in 1521 and became Lord High Chancellor in 1529. The movie, taken from the stage play by Robert Bolt (who also wrote the screenplay), covers the period from 1529 to 1535, when More was executed for treason.

Henry VIII became king in 1509 upon the death of his brother, Arthur. Although Roman Catholic Church law forbade a man to marry his brother's widow, the need to repair relations between England and Spain caused a papal dispensation to be sought and granted. Henry married Catherine of Aragon. When Catherine did not produce a male heir, Henry worried about his dynasty. He asked the pope to dissolve his marriage on the grounds that it was illegal to begin with. When the pope refused, Henry declared that the king was the true head of the Church in England. His marriage to Catherine was set aside, and Henry married Anne Boleyn.

The Act of Succession of 1534 required prominent Englishmen to take an oath accepting the king's supreme authority, even above the pope. More refused to swear the oath. His conscience would not allow him to accept the supremacy of the king over the Church. More had resigned the chancellorship over the issue of the king's marriage dissolution. Through silence and his knowledge of the law, he hoped to avoid being drawn into the political debate.

The movie focuses on the issue of allegiance to the state versus the dictates of one's conscience. In this issue, despite the superb settings and costumes of Tudor England, the film has a timeless quality. A moral individual is pitted against an immoral and often corrupt state.

For the most part, the film accurately portrays the events of More's struggle, even using his own words as recorded at the time. The costuming and settings are typical of Tudor England. The cinematography is also outstanding; note the use of architectural features such as gargoyles and statues of the King's Beasts to set the scene. *A Man for All Seasons* was filmed at the famous Shepperton Studios in London as well as on location at such Tudor sites as Hampton Court.

It is important to note that Thomas More was not a character without flaws. He was not as quiet about the King's "divorce" as the film would suggest. He vehemently hated Protestants and thought that they should be burned as heretics; he wrote volumes on this subject. He also was not as firm a follower of the Pope as the film portrays him. He had written that popes had erred and that a church council was preferable to a pope's authority. The villains of the film, Cromwell and Riche, are also portrayed as much more evil than they were in reality. We have no evidence to believe that Thomas Cromwell was out to get More; he was godfather to the child of Will Roper and More's daughter Margaret after More's death.

This was an honor that would hardly be offered to the Cromwell portrayed in the film. A typical characteristic of feature films is to make the issue of good versus evil very clear-cut and black-and-white. More was not the saint that he is pictured to be, and his antagonists were not nearly the villains as shown.

SYNOPSIS OF THE PLOT

The film opens with Thomas More receiving a message from Cardinal Wolsey requesting his immediate presence. Wolsey questions More as to why he always opposes the cardinal, why he is always bound by conscience and not politics. Wolsey also informs More of his efforts to procure an annulment for the king so that Henry can marry Anne Boleyn. More refuses to offer his help in this effort. When More returns home, he is met by Richard Rich, a young man seeking a position at court. More counsels him to become a teacher and avoid the bribes and corruption of the court.

After what appears to be a passage of several months, Cardinal Wolsey dies. Thomas More is appointed Lord High Chancellor. In a display of pageantry, a flotilla of boats carries King Henry VIII to More's home in Chelsea. Henry has a reason for the visit; he wants More's support for his annulment. More cannot give his support; Henry rushes off to catch the tide. More's wife, Alice, is concerned about her husband's future, but More assures her that he is not the stuff of which martyrs are made. Master Rich appeals to More once again for a job, but he is turned down. Rich then meets with Thomas Cromwell, a government official who is eager for information that could be used against More.

The scene then switches to the convocation of English bishops at Canterbury. A representative of the king reads a document that proclaims the king to be the head of the English Church. More resigns his office as chancellor in protest against this action. More tells his friend Thomas Howard, duke of Norfolk, about his beliefs and his fears. More assures his wife that he will make no statement about the king's actions. He believes that his silence will protect him.

Cromwell is working on painting More as treacherous and uses Rich as a witness. Cromwell tells Norfolk to get More to bless and attend the king's wedding to Anne Boleyn or there could be severe consequences. More does not attend the wedding.

A messenger comes to More's house, which is now bare of furnishings, showing his decline in fortune. More is to appear at court to answer charges. More does appear before Cromwell. Cromwell states that the king is displeased with More but will reinstate him if he accepts the king's religious policies. More refuses, and Cromwell charges him with treason.

More is free to go, but he cannot find a boatman to carry him home. He meets Norfolk, who begs him to give in to the king's wishes. They quarrel and part, their friendship broken. More walks home through a symbolically dark and stormy forest, while Cromwell passes a new act through Parliament that everyone must take an oath to support the king and his marriage.

More finds he cannot in conscience take the oath. He is confined to the Tower of London as a prisoner. Months pass. One night More is taken to Richmond to meet with Cromwell and Norfolk, who is the new Lord High Chancellor. They ask More once more if he will recognize the king's marriage and rights of succession. More refuses once more; he also refuses to give his reasons and objections.

More's family is allowed to visit him in prison after promising to try to persuade him to give in. More refuses once again, and they say farewell for what they know will be the last time. More is brought to trial before Parliament on the charge of high treason. More announces to the assembly that he stands on his silence. The trial becomes a battle of wits and legal knowledge between Cromwell and More. Richard Rich, by now a finely dressed official, is called as a witness; he makes a statement that condemns More. More denies the charge, but realizes that he is a doomed man. More is proclaimed to be guilty and condemned to death. At his execution, More proclaims that he dies the king's good servant, but God's first.

IDEAS FOR CLASS DISCUSSION

An interesting discussion might center around Henry's obsessive desire for a male heir to succeed him. Henry VII had taken over in 1485 after nearly 30 years of civil war. This long period of conflict had been caused by disputes in the line of succession; no doubt, this had been emphasized to his heir, the future Henry VIII. Another discussion topic might be whether an individual who is felt to be a threat to the peace and security of the land should be sacrificed for the greater good. The issue of loyalty to the state and its laws versus the dictates of conscience is one portrayed in many plays and other works of literature. It might be interesting to compare this drama to the Greek drama *Antigone*.

BOOKS AND MATERIALS RELATING TO THIS FILM AND TOPIC

Bolt, Robert. *A Man for All Seasons* (Random House, 1966).

Bridgett, Thomas E. *Life and Writings of Sir Thomas More* (Scholarly Publications, 1976).

Lacey, Robert. *The Life and Times of Henry VIII* (Praeger Publishers, 1972).

Marius, Richard. *Thomas More* (Knopf, 1984).

Williams, Neville. *Henry VIII and His Court* (Macmillan, 1971).

OTHER MEDIA RESOURCES FOR THIS TIME PERIOD

Anne of a Thousand Days (1969, 145 minutes) This is the story of Henry's ill-fated relationship with Anne Boleyn.

Elizabeth (1998, 124 minutes) This film is about Elizabeth I's accession to the throne and her early years as queen. Rated **R**

Henry VIII and His Six Wives (1973, 125 minutes) Henry's unusual marital history is covered in this adaptation of the BBC television series featured on PBS.

Lady Jane (1986, 140 minutes) After the death of Henry's son Edward VI, a schemer tries to get Lady Jane Grey proclaimed as the legitimate heir to the throne.

Luther (1973, 112 minutes) This adaptation of John Osborne's play covers Luther's life from his days as a monk through the Peasant's Rebellion.

A Matter of Conscience: Henry VIII and Thomas More (1972, 30 minutes) Part of the Learning Corporation of America's *Western Civilization: Majesty and Madness* series. A condensation of the film *A Man for All Seasons*, this is designed for classroom use and discussion.

The Private Life of Henry VIII (1933, 97 minutes) This film classic stars Charles Laughton as the king.

The Return of Martin Guerre (1982, 111 minutes) This is an excellent re-creation of peasant life during the sixteenth century. Natalie Zemon Davis, author of the book with the same title, served as the film's historical advisor and has written much on the film's historical accuracy.

Shakespeare in Love (1998, 122 minutes) This Academy Award-winning costume drama takes place during the reign of Queen Elizabeth I. It is notable for its portrayal of Elizabethan theater. One glaring historical error is that the heroine is sent off to a plantation in Virginia long before Jamestown is founded. Rated **R**

UNIT 6

The Reformation

— A MAN FOR ALL SEASONS —

Columbia Pictures Corporation, 1966; directed by Fred Zinnemann

Major Character	Actor/Actress
Sir Thomas More	Paul Scofield
Cardinal Wolsey	Orson Welles
Henry VIII	Robert Shaw
Thomas Cromwell	Leo McKern
Richard Rich	John Hurt
Thomas Howard, Duke of Norfolk	Nigel Davenport
Lady Alice More	Wendy Hiller
Margaret More	Susannah York
Will Roper	Corin Redgrave

WHAT TO WATCH FOR

This film is based on a play by Robert Bolt. The main character, Sir Thomas More, was an extremely well-known scholar in sixteenth-century Europe. More was a noted writer and humanist. He also rose to prominence in the court of King Henry VIII. He became Lord High Chancellor of England, the highest judicial officer of the crown.

At the time when the film begins, around 1530, England (unlike other parts of Europe) had not experienced the Protestant Reformation begun by Martin Luther. A turning point came, however. Henry VIII, desperate for a male heir, wished the pope to dissolve his marriage to Catherine of Aragon so that he could marry Anne Boleyn. When the pope refused, Henry declared that the king, not the pope, was the head of the Church in England.

(continued)

Thomas More could not in conscience accept the king's authority over the pope's. Note in the film More's arguments against the king's actions. Also note how More uses his knowledge of the law to protect himself.

The movie was filmed in England. It contains good images of Tudor England using actual structures from that era, such as Hampton Court Palace and a typical sixteenth-century manor house. The costuming is historically accurate, as are small details such as More's paying the executioner to ensure a swift and accurate fall of the axe.

The cinematography uses camera shots to create certain moods. For example, the power of the Tudor king is conveyed by shots of the stone statues of the King's Beasts. More's journey home alone through a dark and stormy forest symbolizes his fall from power. Watch for other such devices.

Screening Notes

A MAN FOR ALL SEASONS

VOCABULARY

Act of Succession

Act of Supremacy

archbishop of Canterbury

bishop

dynasty

heretic

House of Commons

Lord High Chancellor

Lutheran

Parliament

pope

QUESTIONS BASED ON THE FILM

1. How important was the Thames River in sixteenth-century England? Did you notice any similarities between transportation in Tudor England and today?

_____

_____

_____

_____

2. How does King Henry VIII test the scholarship of More's daughter, Margaret? How does this coincide with and deviate from the standards of learning at that time?

_____

_____

_____

_____

(continued)

3. How does Henry justify his request that his marriage to Catherine of Aragon be dissolved?

_____

_____

_____

_____

_____

4. How does Thomas More use the law to defend himself?

_____

_____

_____

_____

_____

_____

5. What corruptions existed in sixteenth-century government as portrayed in the film?

_____

_____

_____

_____

_____

(continued)

6. The title of this play and film is taken from a passage written by Robert Whittington (around 1520):

> More is a man of an angel's wit and singular learning; I know not his fellow. For where is the man of that gentleness, lowliness, and affability? And as time requireth, a man of marvelous mirth and pastimes; and sometimes of as sad a gravity: a man for all seasons.

How does the film show More in relation to this description? How was he "a man for all seasons"?

_____

_____

_____

_____

_____

_____

_____

TEACHER'S GUIDE

CROMWELL

Columbia Pictures Corporation, 1970; directed
by Ken Hughes, color, 128 minutes

BACKGROUND OF THE FILM

This film is a lavishly costumed spectacle about the
tumultuous period of the English Civil Wars, covering
the years 1640–1653. It is an excellent example of a
film that does well in accurately portraying the battle
scenes, weapons, dress, and building interiors of the
time, but it shows a disregard for historical fact. It
uses the common Hollywood technique of compressing or telescoping time, simplifying events, and using
one character as a focus for the action.

The well-known historians Will and Ariel Durant
consulted on this film, and the settings and props are
well researched. Whitehall Palace as shown in the film
is identical to contemporary paintings of the time,
complete to the checkered pattern on the floor and
the hunting dog lurking near the dining table. Some
of the characters show historically verified characteristics. Charles I speaks with a slight stutter; many of
his speeches are taken from written evidence. Henrietta Maria, by all accounts, was overbearing and stubborn. Prince Rupert did, in fact, bring his poodle
everywhere, although he was a far more respected
and gallant commander than the film portrays him.

It is with the figure of Oliver Cromwell that the
film distorts history the most. Cromwell was a relative unknown, a parliamentary backbencher throughout the early years of the conflict. It was not until his
formation of the New Model Army and the victory
at Naseby in 1645 that he became an important

figure. His name was not included on the list of five
Puritans whom the king tried to arrest in 1642. John
Pym was the acknowledged leader of the Puritans;
it was he who was listened to, not Cromwell, who
rarely spoke in Parliament. To simplify the characters
and plot, Cromwell in this film becomes the personi-
fication of all opposition to the king.

The film also simplifies the issues, making the
supporters of the king the villains as opposed to the
Puritans, who are portrayed in the film as political
liberals. The scene in which Cromwell tells the king
that England should move to a more enlightened form
of government, a democracy, is pure fiction. This was
probably done to give general audiences a clear-cut
case of right and wrong—the popular good guys
versus bad guys theme.

Despite its factual shortcomings, such as Charles
dissolving Parliament to begin the civil war (the Long
Parliament was never dissolved), Cromwell's son
being killed at Naseby (he had died of smallpox years
earlier), and the omission of four years when Cromwell was subduing the Scots and Irish, the film can be
used for its portrayal of the ambience of the time and
as a lesson in viewing skills. Students can compare
their understanding of historical events with the film's
portrayal. They can also perhaps discuss why a film
would consciously change factual evidence.

SYNOPSIS OF THE PLOT

It is the year 1640. Two Puritan leaders, John Pym
and Henry Ireton, try to persuade landowning squire
Oliver Cromwell not to emigrate to America. They
tell Cromwell that Parliament, which has not met for

11 years, may be reconvened; they hint at growing unrest, perhaps a civil war. Cromwell, though fed up with governmental corruption, remains loyal to his king and will not hear of treasonous talk.

In the next scene, common land that has been used by the peasants is sold by the king to gain revenues. A farmworker, John Carter, tries to stop the land transfer, but he is arrested and taken off despite Cromwell's intervention. Later in church, Cromwell is confronted by ornate trappings on the altar. His anger is intense as he is told that this infringement on the simple Puritan style of worship is by order of the king. John Carter returns from his captors, beaten and mutilated.

Meanwhile, the king is dining in his splendid palace and receives the Earl of Strafford from Ireland. Strafford urges the king to seek funds for an army to use against the Scots, who are rebelling. In response, the king is forced to call Parliament into session to raise funds. Cromwell is elected to Parliament. He arrives at Westminster to find the body divided on the issue of money for the king. Some members, particularly the Puritans, want a redress of grievances before voting any money.

To appease Parliament, the king signs an order to execute Strafford. Charles then meets with a group from Parliament to discuss their differences. Urged by his queen, Charles decides to arrest his main opponents in Parliament. Warned ahead of time by the king's advisor, Edward Hyde, the Puritan leaders flee, except for Cromwell. The king enters Parliament and, on seeing that "the birds have flown," dissolves Parliament.

A civil war results. At the first battle, Edgehill, the Parliamentary forces are badly beaten by the superior Royalist troops led by Prince Rupert, the king's nephew. Cromwell decides to raise a new army of handpicked, highly disciplined soldiers. This New Model Army is successful at the battle of Naseby in 1645.

Despite Charles's efforts to raise a Catholic Irish army and to get aid from France, he is defeated and captured by Cromwell. Unfortunately, with victory,

Parliament dissolves into a bickering rabble, and Cromwell finds it necessary to use force to get his way. He goes to negotiate privately with the king to keep England a monarchy, but with certain conditions. Charles pretends to study the terms, but secretly he negotiates with Cromwell's enemies to begin a second civil war.

The treachery of the king forces Cromwell to put Charles on trial for treason. Charles is found guilty and condemned to death. On January 30, 1649, wearing an extra shirt so as not to shiver in the cold, Charles meets his death as a martyr. A Commonwealth is established under the rule of Parliament, and Cromwell returns home. The Commonwealth is a failure; Parliament cannot rule. Cromwell is offered the crown, which he scornfully rejects. Later, Cromwell visits Parliament and, disgusted with its corruption, orders the army to eject the members. The film ends with Cromwell seated in Parliament declaring that England will be a great nation even if he has to rule it himself. A narrator tells us that, indeed, Cromwell did rule as Lord Protector and was responsible for England's increased greatness as a nation.

IDEAS FOR CLASS DISCUSSION

As stated above, this film particularly lends itself to a discussion of critical viewing and the devices that Hollywood uses in presenting a historical event to a popular audience. What the film does well, such as costuming and ambience, it does very well. It is weaker when it tries to simplify events by telescoping time and characters. A good topic for class discussion would be the reasons why films "change" history. Do filmmakers do it for logical reasons of clarity and audience appeal? A discussion on the truly complex issues of the English Civil Wars would also be profitable. What does the film leave out, and why?

BOOKS AND MATERIALS RELATING TO THIS FILM AND TOPIC

Ashley, Maurice. *Oliver Cromwell and His World* (G.P. Putnam Sons, 1972).

Cowie, Leonard W. *The Trial and Execution of Charles I* (G.P. Putnam Sons, 1972).

Fraser, Antonia. *Cromwell, the Lord Protector* (Alfred A. Knopf, 1973).

Ollard, Richard. *This War Without an Enemy, A History of the English Civil Wars* (Atheneum, 1976).

Young, Peter. *Oliver Cromwell and His Times* (Arco Publishing, 1962).

OTHER MEDIA RESOURCES FOR THIS TIME PERIOD

The Last Valley (1971, 128 minutes) Written by James Clavell, this film is set in the destructive period of the Thirty Years War.

The Puritan Revolution: Cromwell and the Rise of Parliamentary Democracy (1970, 33 minutes) Produced by the Learning Corporation of America, this film condenses the 1970 *Cromwell* into 33 minutes by adding narration. This is a good alternative to the feature-length film.

Restoration (1995, 117 minutes) This lavish costume drama of the court of Charles II gives a good picture of the time period, including such things as the plague and the Great Fire of London. It does contain several scenes that are explicitly sexual; use selectively. Rated **R**

The Three Musketeers (1974, 107 minutes) and *The Four Musketeers* (1975, 108 minutes) Both are directed by Richard Lester, and both capture the swashbuckling flavor of the Dumas stories as well as conditions in the France of Louis XIV.

Winstanley (1975, 95 minutes) A unique film, this tells the story of a "Digger" community in the period just following the English Civil Wars. The filmmakers have attempted to achieve total historical accuracy. The characters are dirty and disheveled, with bad teeth and complexions—hardly the typical Hollywood image of the seventeenth century, or any century, for that matter.

CROMWELL

Columbia Pictures, 1970; directed by Ken Hughes

Major Character	Actor/Actress
Oliver Cromwell	Richard Harris
King Charles I	Alec Guinness
Queen Henrietta Maria	Dorothy Tutin
Earl of Manchester	Robert Morley
Prince Rupert	Timothy Dalton
John Carter	Frank Finlay
Earl of Strafford	Patrick Wymark
Sir Edward Hyde	Nigel Stock
Henry Ireton	Michael Jayston

WHAT TO WATCH FOR

This film is an excellent example of how Hollywood dilutes and condenses historical events. Watch for gaps of time that are unexplained. Also look for historical mistakes, such as when the film presents Charles's dissolution of Parliament as the beginning of the civil war. (In reality, Parliament was not officially dissolved until 1660.) Watch also how the complex issues that caused the English Civil Wars are oversimplified. Based on your knowledge of seventeenth-century issues, why might a film for a general audience need to do this?

The character of Cromwell is portrayed as far too important in the early years of the civil war. Cromwell was a relative unknown in Parliament. He did not assume any leadership role until he formed the New Model Army with Thomas Fairfax. The other characters in the film are fairly accurate according to descriptions of them written at that time. Queen Henrietta Maria was very firm with Charles about his role as king. Remember, she was French; French kings were absolute monarchs,

(continued)

with no Parliament to restrict their wishes. Many of Charles's speeches are also taken from historical records.

The costumes, scenery, weapons, and battle scenes are quite accurate. Note the large and primitive firearms; the guns are so heavy that their barrels must be supported by poles. Guns were not highly accurate in the seventeenth century. Foot soldiers with pikes and swordsmen on horseback (the cavalry) were still the most effective fighting force. The movie was filmed in Spain rather than England, because Spain had open land without twentieth-century intrusions such as airplane jet trails and power-plant smokestacks.

Screening Notes

The Crises of the Seventeenth Century

CROMWELL

VOCABULARY

Anglican

Commonwealth

Magna Carta

New Model Army

Parliament

Puritan

Reformation

Roundhead

Royalist

treason

QUESTIONS BASED ON THE FILM

1. What conditions in England have made Cromwell plan to leave for America?

   _____

   _____

   _____

2. Why does the king fence in and sell the common land?

   _____

   _____

3. What causes Cromwell's fury in the Puritan church?

   _____

   _____

(continued)

4. Why is the king forced to call Parliament into session in 1640?

_____

_____

5. Note the scene in which parliamentary leaders meet with King Charles at his palace. Can you find any statements in the film that are totally inconsistent with seventeenth-century ideas of government and who has the right to rule?

_____

_____

_____

_____

6. Why are the Parliamentary forces so badly defeated at Edgehill? What happens to turn the tide of the war in their favor?

_____

_____

_____

7. Why is Charles put on trial for treason? What has driven Cromwell and his supporters to this act?

_____

_____

_____

(continued)

8. It has been said that Charles's manner of death did more to uphold the monarchy than anything he ever did during his life. In viewing the execution scene (which is, by all accounts, accurate), do you feel this is true? Why?

_____

_____

_____

_____

9. Why does Cromwell eject the members of Parliament in 1653? How is England governed from 1653 to 1660?

_____

_____

10. The film omits the nearly four years between the execution of Charles and Cromwell's forcing out Parliamentary members in 1653. Historically, what was Cromwell doing during that time? Why would the Irish actor Richard Harris, who played Cromwell, say that he would not play the part of Cromwell in Ireland for fear of finding a bomb under his bed?

_____

_____

_____

_____

—————— TEACHER'S GUIDE ——————

NAPOLEON

A reconstruction from Zoetrope Studios, 1927; directed by Abel Gance, black and white (some versions are tinted and toned), 235 minutes. The 1981 reconstruction was done by Kevin Brownlow.

BACKGROUND OF THE FILM

Napoléon vu par Abel Gance is a historic film for two reasons. First, from a cinematic viewpoint, it is innovative and revolutionary. Second, from the viewpoint of history, it provides an insight into how the French regard their Revolution of 1789 and Napoléon.

The film premiered in 1927 at the Théâtre National de l'Opéra in Paris. It was received enthusiastically by a cheering audience, which included a young army officer named Charles de Gaulle. With its innovations, the film was expected to revolutionize the film industry. Instead, the film disappeared for months. When it *was* released in the United States and other countries, it was in a shortened, poorly edited version minus the creative innovations for which the film had won its initial acclaim. Due to the sound revolution facing the motion picture industry with the release of *The Jazz Singer, Napoleon* was deemed too expensive to show. It was a silent film and required three projectors for the triptychs, a three-scene process that Gance called Polyvision.

British film historian Kevin Brownlow became interested in *Napoleon* as a schoolboy. He has dedicated years to the reconstruction of *Napoleon* and public recognition of the genius of Abel Gance. His 1981 reconstruction, produced by Francis Ford Coppola with music composed and conducted by Carmine Coppola, is the most common version of *Napoleon* available in the United States.

Abel Gance lavished extraordinary amounts of time and money on his *Napoleon,* which was to be only the first of six films spanning Bonaparte's life. Many of the locations were the actual sites where the events had taken place. Gance was careful to prepare the costumes and settings with accuracy and detail. The hundreds of hired extras were inspired to believe deeply in the project and throw themselves completely into the spirit of the time and event. Whereas most historical films were static and tableau-like, Gance wanted dynamic action to propel audiences into the scenes. A camera was strapped to the back of a horse for the chase scene in Corsica. A camera swung on a huge pendulum to give the impression of a storm rocking the National Convention in the heat of an upheaval during the Revolution. Polyvision was Gance's most startling creation— three projectors were used to show a triptych of images on three screens, 30 years before Cinerama used this same technique.

Although historically many of the sequences portrayed are pure fantasy or fiction, the spirit of the revolutionary period captured by the film is important. Gance felt that emotion, and transfer of emotion from the screen to the audience, was all-important and worth any sacrifice to authenticity.* The film also captures the mythical-symbolic essence of the French Revolution and Napoléon as perceived by the French

*See Kevin Brownlow, *Napoleon, Abel Gance's Classic Film,* Alfred A. Knopf, 1983, p. 35.

people so many years later. For high-school students in the United States who have grown up with stories about George Washington, Benjamin Franklin, and Paul Revere's ride, this demonstrates that other countries also have national icons and symbols—legends that become larger than life in the retelling. Gance's attitude toward the figure of Napoléon and the film can be best expressed in a quotation taken from the original program from the film's premiere: "Napoléon was a climax in his generation, which in turn was a climax in time. And cinema, for me, is the climax of life."

Despite its length, this film can be a valuable resource for both the history of film and the history of the French Revolution.

SYNOPSIS OF THE PLOT

The film begins at the Franciscan-run military college of Brienne, where Napoléon is a pupil. The boys are engaged in a snowball fight. Napoléon is commanding the defense of his snow fort, showing military genius and courage at an early age. One of the teachers, M. Pichegu, states that Napoléon will go far. We see a premonition of Napoléon's future when the pupils study St. Helena, a small island.

Napoléon is persecuted by his classmates, and his pet eagle is set free by two boys. Napoléon attacks his classmates in an enormous pillow fight, dramatized by Gance in a nine-part split screen. The monks send Napoléon into the snow; as he lies weeping on a cannon, his eagle returns, a symbol of his great destiny.

Years later, in Paris in 1789, the French Revolution has begun. A young army officer, Rouget de Lisle, has brought a song, "La Marseillaise," to the leaders of the Revolution. Danton presents de Lisle to the crowd in the Assembly, and his anthem whips the crowd to a frenzied passion. Napoléon, a young lieutenant, thanks de Lisle: "Your hymn will save many a cannon."

Napoléon returns with his sister to his homeland, Corsica. A leader of Corsica, Paoli, has aligned his island with the English. Napoléon feels that he must pledge Corsica to the cause of the French Revolution. Napoléon fails, and he is outlawed. In a dramatic chase scene, he makes it to the coast with a captured tricolor. Napoléon sets out to sea in a small boat, using the tricolor as a sail. A violent storm assails Napoléon at sea, while at the same time the Convention is beset by a violent storm of a political nature.

Napoléon is saved by his brothers and pulled aboard the brig *Le Hasard*. The rest of the family is rescued as Napoléon's eagle lands on the mast, symbolic once more of his destiny. The Bonaparte family now takes France as their only homeland.

The scene then shifts to the siege of Toulon in 1793. The port of Toulon is controlled by the English under Admiral Hood. Napoléon is sent to Toulon to plan an attack on the English. He is first ridiculed but later accepted by the new commander, General Dugommier. At night, in a torrential downpour, Napoléon assaults the English positions. He is successful; the British withdraw, but they burn the French fleet as they leave. After the battle, Napoléon is found sleeping with his head on a drum guarded by the eagle of his destiny.

In Part Two, Napoléon returns to Paris to find the city in the middle of the Reign of Terror. Marat is killed by Charlotte Corday to avenge the Girondins. A Committee of Public Safety is set up with Robespierre, Saint-Just (played by Abel Gance), and Couthon as leaders. When Napoléon refuses to take the command of Paris, he is imprisoned. Danton goes to the guillotine, and Josephine de Beauharnais is also imprisoned. During Thermidor (July 1794), the Terror subsides and Robespierre is condemned. Josephine and Napoléon are freed, but Napoléon, who still refuses to fight the Royalists, is sent to the Office of Topography in disgrace. Napoléon makes up plans for the invasion of Italy, but they are rejected. He is forced to use them to cover holes in his window.

Finally, Napoléon is called upon to save the Republic. When Royalist forces threaten the government, Barras enlists Napoléon to take command. In Vendémiaire (October 1794), Napoléon defeats the Royalists and becomes a hero. As celebrations occur all over Paris, Napoléon attends the Bal de Victimes, held for former prisoners of the Terror. Josephine also attends, and the two meet.

When Napoléon is appointed commander of the Armies of the Interior, he orders all weapons turned in. A young boy meets with Napoléon and pleads to keep his father's sword. Napoléon agrees, and the boy's mother, Josephine, comes to thank him. Napoléon fumbles and fusses over her; it is clear that he is in love. Josephine makes a deal with her protector, Barras; if Napoléon is appointed to command the Army of the Alps, she will marry Bonaparte. Barras is anxious to be rid of Josephine and agrees to the deal. Napoléon, absorbed in his plans to conquer Italy, almost misses his own wedding. He finally appears and pushes the ceremony to a quick completion.

Napoléon bids farewell to Josephine and hurries off to join his army. Before he leaves Paris, he visits the empty Convention. He is visited by the ghosts of the Convention, and Napoléon proclaims that he will strive for the Universal Republic.

Napoléon's army is encamped in the foothills of the Alps; they are ill-equipped and poorly fed. The officers believe that Napoléon is a young upstart. Napoléon wins over both officers and soldiers with his leadership and vision. The army begins its march into Italy, with Napoléon's eagle of destiny hovering overhead.

IDEAS FOR CLASS DISCUSSION

Napoléon has become a symbol for the French people of their past greatness and European dominance. A good topic for discussion would be how this movie portrays Napoléon and his rise to power. The interesting technique that Gance employs to demonstrate the chaos of the Convention during the Revolution is a good topic for discussion. Was it as stormy and turbulent as Gance portrays it? A good discussion might also involve the circumstances that would allow someone like Napoléon to rise above his beginnings. Remember, he was not French. Would he have been as great in another era?

BOOKS AND MATERIALS RELATING TO THIS FILM AND TOPIC

Brinton, Crane. *A Decade of Revolution, 1789–1799* (Harper & Row, 1934).

Brownlow, Kevin. *Napoleon, Abel Gance's Classic Film* (Alfred A. Knopf, 1983).

Cronin, Vincent. *Napoleon Bonaparte, An Intimate Biography* (William Morrow, 1972).

Ludwig, Emil. *Napoleon* (Liveright Publishing, 1954).

Rude, George. *Robespierre, Portrait of a Revolutionary Democrat* (Viking Press, 1975).

OTHER MEDIA RESOURCES FOR THIS TIME PERIOD

La Marseillaise (1937, French, 131 minutes) Directed by Jean Renoir, this is a documentary-style story of the storming of the Bastille.

The Madness of King George (1994, 107 minutes) This well-acted film is about the mental illness of King George III of England and the efforts of his son (the future Prince Regent and George IV) to seize power.

Napoleon (1955, 115 minutes) An illustrious cast, including Orson Welles, Yves Montand, and Erich von Stroheim, appear in a fairly bland film biography.

A Tale of Two Cities (1935, 121 minutes) This is a classic Hollywood film starring Ronald Coleman; it remains true to the Dickens novel. Basil Rathbone is a despicable marquis.

That Hamilton Woman (1941, 128 minutes) This film about Admiral Nelson and his affair with Lady Hamilton stars Laurence Olivier and Vivien Leigh; it carries the story through Nelson's death at the Battle of Trafalgar.

Waterloo (1971, 123 minutes) Rod Steiger plays Napoléon, Christopher Plummer is Wellington, and Orson Welles is Louis XVIII. The battle scenes are extraordinary.

NAPOLEON

1981 Kevin Brownlow reconstruction of film by Zoetrope Studios, 1927; directed by Abel Gance

Major Character	Actor/Actress
Napoléon (as a boy)	Vladimir Roudenko
Napoléon Bonaparte	Albert Dieudonné
Josephine de Beauharnais	Gina Manès
Tristan Fleury	Nicolas Koline
Danton	Alexandre Koubitzky
Marat	Antonin Artaud
Robespierre	Edmond Van Daële
Couthon	M'Viguier
Louis Saint-Just	Abel Gance
Rouget de Lisle	Harry Krimer

WHAT TO WATCH FOR

This remarkable silent film was first released in 1927. It contained innovations many years ahead of its time. Because of its length, expense (it required three projectors), and the recent success of *The Jazz Singer,* a sound picture, *Napoleon* did not fare well. It was shown in many cities in an abbreviated, poorly edited form. British film historian Kevin Brownlow discovered several reels of this film as a schoolboy. Since then, he has devoted years to the rehabilitation of this work as a masterpiece. Brownlow's 1981 reconstruction was shown in major U.S. cities, with live orchestra accompaniment, to wide acclaim.

Remember that this is a silent film and that many of the actors were used to the stage. Their gestures and emotions might seem too flamboyant to a modern audience. Yet, these devices helped explain to a 1927 audience what was happening without using too many subtitles, which can be distracting. Notice the faces of the

(continued)

many extras. Gance used nonprofessionals, but he inspired them to put themselves into the spirit of the time and place. Gance used French schoolboys actually from Brienne for the scenes at Napoléon's school. He used Corsican peasants while shooting on the Bonaparte family's island homeland. The sans-culottes were Renault auto workers who happened to be out on strike.

Notice the camera innovations. Gance used the first hand-held camera; he even strapped one to a horse for the chase scene on Corsica. Note also the famous double storm sequence, where Napoléon is in his small boat at sea while the Convention is being rocked by violent political unrest. This sequence was produced by swinging a camera on a giant pendulum. Triptychs used three screens to show the movie as a panorama. This predated Cinerama, a similar technique, by almost 30 years.

Napoleon is significant for showing how the French regard the Revolution and rise of Napoléon in a symbolic, almost reverent way. It is a human drama of passion, a significant part of the French people's history. Often in the retelling, such events and figures seem superhuman. *How* an event is portrayed is often as important as *what* is being portrayed. Gance freely admitted that he had changed and embellished history for the sake of capturing the emotion of the Revolution. Keep in mind that the full title of this film is *Napoléon vu par Abel Gance*, or *Napoléon As Seen by Abel Gance*.

Screening Notes

NAPOLEON

VOCABULARY

Danton

Declaration of the Rights of Man and of
the Citizen

Girondins

guillotine

Jacobins

La Marseillaise

Marat

National Convention

Reign of Terror

Robespierre

sans-culottes

Thermidorean Reaction

the Vendée

Vendémiaire

QUESTIONS BASED ON THE FILM

1. Tristan Fleury first appears as a kitchen worker at Brienne. As he appears throughout the film, how does Fleury represent the figure of the common man in his relationship with Napoléon?

_____

_____

_____

_____

_____

_____

(continued)

2. How does Gance use foreshadowing in the film?

_____

_____

_____

_____

_____

_____

3. Compare the sans-culottes with the French nobility. How is each group portrayed?

_____

_____

_____

_____

_____

_____

4. How are the English stereotyped in this film?

_____

_____

_____

_____

_____

_____

(continued)

5. What is the significance of the insurrection of August 10, 1792?

_____

_____

_____

_____

_____

_____

6. How does the scene with the ghosts of the Revolution in the Convention show how many French people justified (and still justify) Napoléon's conquests?

_____

_____

_____

_____

_____

_____

7. How did Napoléon inspire such confidence and spirit in his soldiers? How does the film portray this?

_____

_____

_____

_____

_____

_____

The Industrial Revolution

TEACHER'S GUIDE

GERMINAL

Renn Productions, 1993; directed by Claude Berri, color, 170 minutes. In French with English subtitles; rated **R** for intense depiction of suffering, class conflict, and sexual content.

BACKGROUND OF THE FILM

Perhaps no other event changed the life of the average European more than the Industrial Revolution of the early nineteenth century, when hundreds of thousands of peasants moved from rural to urban areas to work in mills, factories, and mines. With agricultural improvements and labor-saving devices, a large labor force was no longer needed to work the land. People were forced to seek work elsewhere, but a growing urban population meant that the supply of labor exceeded the demand; wages were accordingly low. Industrial areas grew so rapidly that they were built beyond municipal regulations. Companies thus had the freedom to control housing and other amenities without restriction. Since housing was in short supply, cheap tenements were constructed in close proximity to the factories to shelter the workers. This created communities that were overcrowded and lacking in sanitation.

Industrial workers were totally at the mercy of the factory owners. In rural societies during hard economic times, the food supply was close at hand; even artisans could engage in some subsistence farming to tide their families over. Urban or mine workers, on the other hand, were wholly dependent on wages for food and shelter. Those wages were controlled by the industrialists, whose biggest concern was to cover capital and raw material costs, make profits, and justify factory construction and expensive machinery costs. In the early years of industrialism, any sort of worker collaboration was considered a violation of free trade. Laws existed that restricted workers from forming any kind of cooperative organization. It was generally assumed that any action taken against an employer would result in mass firings, and there were enough people unemployed to readily replace those workers who did not toe the company line. In France, the Le Chapelier law was passed in 1791, forbidding workers to organize. This law lasted for three quarters of a century.

It is against this background that Émile Zola wrote *Germinal,* his classic novel about French coal miners during the Second Empire of Napoléon III, on which this film was based. During the rule of Napoléon III (1852–1870), France went through its industrial revolution. Between 1853 and 1864, French exports doubled. Although the Le Chapelier law had not been repealed, Napoléon III allowed labor unions; it was even legal for workers to go on strike. This period of industrial growth was one of prosperity for some, notably the bourgeoisie, but it was also one of hardship for many workers who fell victim to the downturns in France's economic cycles.

Zola actually traveled to a poor mining district of France to observe firsthand the living conditions of the workers. *Germinal* was written in a style that became a genre known as *naturalism,* for its accurate portrayal of contemporary life and living conditions and its underlying belief that individuals caught in negative social environments had very little chance of breaking free.

There are a few inaccuracies in both the book and the film. The age and family tree of the main character, Étienne Lantier, date the setting at about 1867. However, the worst abuses of women and children in the mines had been corrected by the French government by this time. The conditions depicted in the book and film are more representative of those found in the early years of the Industrial Revolution. The Russian anarchist Souvarine is a fictional character based on Mikhail Bakunin, who was at that time developing his views and moving toward his vocal opposition to Marx over issues of leadership and worker autonomy. This resistance (sometimes called the Battle of the Giants) led to the dissolution of the First International Working Men's Association, which had been founded in 1864. Despite the portrayal of abuses already ameliorated, *Germinal* is a novel that captures the terrible trials endured by the people during a time of economic dislocation, when workers were still viewed as commodities and not as active participants in the economic growth and development of their nation.

The film also reflects the mood and tone of the novel. It clearly represents the conditions of the early Industrial Revolution in Europe and the great differences between the almost obscenely wealthy capitalists and the workers who supported such riches with their labor. Director Claude Berri worked hard to achieve an accurate period look for his film, using an abandoned village built in 1904 as a set. The interior shots of the mine were filmed on a set consisting of 400 meters of tunnels, constructed in an iron and steel plant. To play the important role of Étienne Lantier, Berri coaxed a popular French musician who was also an active Socialist. The role of the miner Toussaint Maheu was played by a very popular French actor, Gérard Depardieu, the star of such films as *The Return of Martin Guerre*, *The Count of Montecristo,* and *Balzac*. One criticism made when the film came out was that Depardieu looked too well fed to play the role of a starving nineteenth-century miner.

The film is very true to the novel, using the same dialogue and plot line. Teachers should be warned that there is one scene of sexual intercourse approximately 35 minutes into the film, which can be skipped over. There is also a rather graphic scene of violence in which the enraged miners' wives castrate the dead body of the shopkeeper Magrait. This, too, can be skipped over without a loss of the story line. Despite its **R** rating, this film is well worth the effort to use and can easily be sampled for classroom use.

SYNOPSIS OF THE PLOT

The film opens at the Voreux Mine at night. Étienne Lantier, an unemployed mechanic, stops by the mine to look for work. He meets Bonnemort, an old miner who now works above ground with the horses, and learns of Bonnemort's near-death escapes when employed below.

The scene switches to the village home of the Maheu family. The family is getting up to work in the mine. There is little food, and the coffee is made with yesterday's grounds. The father, daughter, and two sons go off to work as Bonnemort comes in from the night shift. At the mine, Toussaint Maheu learns that one of his haulers, Fleurance, has died and needs to be replaced. Catherine runs off to find Étienne, even though haulers are usually girls. Étienne descends into the mine with Maheu and Catherine, and they work their vein of coal. (Note for students the mine horses being used below; many never saw daylight, living only in the mines.)

From the depths of the mine, the scene abruptly switches to the estate of the Grégoire family. Maheu's wife, Maheude, arrives with her younger children to beg for charity. The Grégoires are amazed that she has seven children. Their daughter, Cécile, gives Maheude some clothing, but the Grégoires refuse her request for money. Maheude goes to the shopkeeper Magrait and asks for credit; he refuses unless she sends him Catherine as payment.

In the mine, the engineer, Négrel, is furious with the timbering done by the miners. He accuses the miners of shoddy work just to get extra carts of coal. He fines Maheu three francs. The mine owners would like to pay separately for timbering but pay less per cart of coal. After work, Étienne and Maheu stop at an inn run by an ex-miner, Rasseneur. They discuss working conditions and wish that a labor organizer named Pluchart were there, because "he makes bosses tremble." Étienne finds a room at Rasseneur's. The Maheu family goes home, and they wash the coal dust off in a wooden tub in the middle of the floor of their house. (There is a brief scene of nudity here, as well as a scene where Maheu and his wife have intercourse, which can be skipped over.) Catherine goes off with a miner named Chaval, who buys a ribbon for her bonnet and then drags her into the woods for "payment." (This entire segment lasts approximately five minutes and can easily be skipped.)

At the inn, Rasseneur tells Étienne about the International Working Men's Association; it has been founded in London, and many are joining. A worker named Souvarine criticizes Étienne's and Rasseneur's idealism. Souvarine believes that the present society must be destroyed, while Étienne wants workers to organize to build a better world legally.

The annual village fair is held. (Note with students the forms of entertainment.) Zacharie Maheu is engaged to Philomène, and Maheude is unhappy about the loss of her son's wages for the family. Étienne tries to win support for a fund that will support miners in case of a strike. He agrees to board with the Maheu family since Zacharie is moving out.

There is a cave-in at the mine and Jeanlin is injured. The management blames the miners. Maheude complains about her children, saying, "Why have children if they don't work?" Catherine has gone off with Chaval; her wages are lost to the family. At Rasseneur's, the miners discuss a strike. Souverine says that the mine owners would welcome a strike—it will save them money. Pluchart writes that it is too soon to strike. He wants the miners to join the International. Souverine continues to argue against Marxism and for anarchism. The mining company announces a new policy: Timbering will be paid for separately, and the price of coal per cart will be lowered. Maheu receives his pay; it is very low. He is also called into the manager's office, where he is told

that his father's pension is being reviewed. He is warned to stay out of politics or he will regret it. Étienne gathers the workers and calls for a strike.

At a luncheon party at the manager Hennebeau's home, the overseer tells him that there is a strike at Le Voreux. The conversation at the luncheon turns to the economics of the time and the justification for lowering wages. The feeling is that the miners will just drown their problems in drink. Cécile Grégorie is engaged to Négrel, Hennebeau's nephew. (Note with students the difference in engagements between Zacharie and Philomène and Cécile and Paul Négrel. Zacharie's parents view his marriage as an economic disaster to their family, and there is no joy.)

A delegation of miners meets with Hennebeau, who tells them that they are being misled by false promises. He lists the many benefits that the company gives them. He states that "a strike is a disaster for everyone." Despite the manager's arguments, the miners go on strike. Étienne pulls the miners together at a meeting and encourages them to fight for justice. They agree that they must close other mines in the area as well. At Jean-Bart, Chaval tries to get the miners to join in the strike, but there is violent disagreement. Deneulin, the manager, comes to Jean-Bart and convinces the miners that an increase in wages would bankrupt him. The Jean-Bart miners go back to work.

The Voreux miners go to Jean-Bart and try to stop all work. They destroy the miners' lamps and wreck the boilers. The lift cables are cut, and the miners have to escape the pit by ladders. The Voreux miners and their families march back to the village singing the "Marseillaise." At the village, they break into Magrait's shop. When he tries to escape, he falls from the roof and is killed. The enraged women from whom Magrait has demanded sexual favors castrate him. Catherine warns the mob that the gendarme have arrived to keep the peace.

Étienne is forced to go into hiding. In the miners' village, it is winter. One of the Maheu children dies. Maheu tells Étienne that he misses his pit. There is a rumor that the mine owners are hiring Belgians.

Étienne begins to doubt that they should ever have gone on strike. He tells Rasseneur, "Our starved bodies will be more useful than your dumb politics."

Soldiers are sent to Le Voreux to protect the Belgian workers. The miners march to the mine, but the soldiers refuse to let them through. When Négrel tries to get the miners to stop and talk, they throw stones at the soldiers, who then fire into the crowd. Maheu is killed.

A notice is posted that the mine will reopen. The owners state that issues needing improvement will be looked at and that they will aim for justice whenever possible. Maheude doesn't want anyone to go back to work; she asks, "Why is the price of justice so high?" Étienne is blamed for the failure of the strike. He writes that nothing can be changed, and that the rich will always live off the weak. He agrees to go to work in the pit with Catherine.

Meanwhile, Souvarine is sabotaging the mine. The mine is flooded, and the cage shaft collapses, trapping many of the miners below—including Catherine, Étienne, and Chaval. Hennebeau arrives; Négrel informs him of the events. A rescue effort is begun to bring the miners out of another pit opening; some are able to escape. Négrel leads a group of rescuers, including Zacharie, to find the miners who are still trapped by cave-ins. As the rescuers are working, coal damp (methane gas) causes an explosion, and Zacharie is killed.

The Grégoires arrive at the Maheu home with baskets of food. No one is home except Bonnemort, whose mind has gone. Cécile is left alone with Bonnemort, and he strangles her.

At the mine, the rescuers break through and find Étienne and Catherine. Catherine is dead; Étienne is barely alive.

In the final scene, Étienne passes by the mine as he leaves the area. Maheude is dressed as a miner. Jeanlin is also working. Maheude says that the other children will work when they are old enough. She doesn't blame Étienne for the deaths, but says that everyone has been to blame. As Étienne walks away from the mine, he predicts the eventual victory of the workers and a better world for the disadvantaged.

IDEAS FOR CLASS DISCUSSION

This film provides a rich resource for class discussion. Note the juxtaposition of scenes of the miners and their wretched living conditions with scenes of the wealthy bourgeoisie. Also note that the capitalists always have a justification for their rate of pay. This would lend itself very well to a discussion of Riccardo's "Iron Law of Wages," focusing on the "wage fund" portion of Adam Smith's minimum price determination.* Point out how horrified the Grégoires are that Maheude has seven children; look for other examples of the recurrent theme that it is the workers themselves, with their lack of self-control, who cause their own problems. The concept of collective action versus the anarchism espoused by Souvarine is illustrated in the discussions in the inn. The working conditions in the mine are accurate for the nineteenth century, although by mid-century (the time in which this film is set), laws restricted the employment of women and children below ground. Discuss with students that, although working conditions are certainly safer and better in most places today, the differences between rich and poor are not any less dramatic. Twenty-first-century corporate executives receive astronomical salaries, as well as many perks such as private jets and memberships in exclusive clubs.

*David Riccardo (1772–1823) was a British political economist who wrote that if wages were left to the laws of supply and demand, they would naturally fall to subsistence level. Paying the workers more would cause them to have more children, thus destroying any benefit a higher wage would give them.

BOOKS AND MATERIALS RELATING TO THIS FILM AND TOPIC

Dickens, Charles. *Hard Times* (Penguin Classics, 1985).

Engels, Frederick. *The Condition of the Working Class in England: From Personal Observation and Authentic Source* (Stanford University Press, 1994 reprint).

Hart, Roger. *English Life in the Nineteenth Century* (G. P. Putnams Sons, 1971).

Kelly, Alfred. *The German Worker: Autobiographies from the Age of Industrialization* (University of California Press, 1987).

King, Steven, and Geoffrey Timmins. *Making Sense of the Industrial Revolution: English Economy and Society, 1700–1850* (Manchester University Press, 2001).

Traugott, Mark, ed. *The French Worker: Autobiographies of the Early Industrial Era* (University of California Press, 1993).

OTHER MEDIA RESOURCES FOR THIS TIME PERIOD

The Great Train Robbery (1979, 111 minutes) Based on the Michael Crichton book, this film recounts an actual event in Victorian England; fun and fast-moving.

How Green Was My Valley (1941, 118 minutes) This film, which won the Academy Award for Best Picture, tells about the plight of Welsh coal miners in the twentieth century, whose working conditions have changed little since the Industrial Revolution.

Modern Times (1936, 89 minutes, semi-silent) A Chaplin film that pits man against machine. The only sound is the clang of the machinery.

Nicholas Nickleby (1947, 108 minutes) One of many Dickens novels that portrays Victorian England as a backdrop for a morality drama.

Oliver! (1968, 153 minutes) Academy Award-winning musical based on the novel by Charles Dickens. It shows the opulence of Victorian England as well as the seamier side of life.

Pandaemonium (2000, 125 minutes) BBC made-for-television film that details the relationship between Romantic poets Samuel Taylor Coleridge and William Wordsworth; set during the end of the eighteenth century, as industrialism and political agitation are occurring in England.

GERMINAL

Renn Productions, 1993; directed by Claude Berri

Major Character	Actor/Actress
Maheude	Miou-Miou
Étienne Lantier	Renaud
Vincent Maheu dit Bonnemort	Jean Carmet
Catherine Maheu	Judith Henry
Chaval	Jean-Roger Milo
Toussaint Maheu	Gérard Depardieu
Souvarine	Laurent Terzieff
Rasseneur	Jean-Pierre Bisson
Phillipe Hennebeau	Jacques Dacqmine
Madame Hennebeau	Anny Duperey
Maigrat	Gérard Croce
Paul Négrel	Frédéric van den Driessche
Madame Grégoire	Annick Alane
Leon Grégoire	Pierre Lafont
Cécile Grégoire	Cécile Bois

WHAT TO WATCH FOR

Germinal offers a clear picture of working and living conditions during the Industrial Revolution. (By the time frame of this film, however, women and children were usually no longer employed in the mines themselves, working above ground instead.) The film is based on a novel of the same name by the French writer Émile Zola, who was greatly concerned about social and economic justice. The story takes place during the Second Empire in France under Napoléon III. It is set around the year 1867, when the emperor's popularity was declining. At this time, the

(continued)

International Working Men's Association was being formed by Karl Marx and others in London. However, the anarchists were also beginning to promote extreme opposition to economic injustice rather than worker collectives or state rules. The character of Souvarine represents the anarchist point of view. Note the discussions in the inn among Étienne Lantier, Rasseneur, and Souvarine. Each has specific ways of dealing with the miners' situation and growing discontent.

Notice the juxtaposition between scenes of the miners' misery and the wealth of the bourgeois (middle-class) managers. The workers blame the bourgeousie (middle classes) for exploiting them, ignoring their safety concerns, and gouging them for rent, food, and manufactured goods. The bourgeousie blame the miners and their families for the miners' poverty. They ask the workers why they have so many children and why, instead of saving, they drink away their wages. Note the arguments each side uses to justify its position. The miners feel that the owners and managers are living off the sweat of their labor. The managers feel higher wages would bankrupt them. Deneulin, the manager of Jean-Bart, tells the miners that before they make a living, he must make a living.

Girl Dragging Coal Tubs

The living and working conditions shown in the film are accurate. In the mines, people spent long hours underground, working in terrible conditions of great heat and moisture. Coal damp, or firedamp, was a constant fear. Black lung disease (suffered by Bonnemort) was an occupational hazard. Methane gas could explode

(continued)

from the flame in the miners' lamps. Mine horses were lowered into the mines as shown in the film; they often spent the rest of their lives below ground. Housing for workers lacked running water and proper sanitation. Maheude has to get water from a communal pump and heats bath water outside over a fire. Although such primitive living conditions do exist in some parts of the world today, they were common in Europe in the nineteenth century. Eventually, many governments began to take responsibility for the welfare of their citizens. Reforms were made to provide adequate housing, sanitation, working conditions, and wages. However, this often took many years of protest and organization by the working class themselves and their supporters.

Screening Notes

The Industrial Revolution

GERMINAL

VOCABULARY

anarchism

black lung disease

firedamp/coal damp

gendarme

International Working Men's Association

Karl Marx

sabotage

scab labor

QUESTIONS BASED ON THE FILM

1. What is Maheu's reaction when he finds out that his hauler, Fleurance, has died?

   _____

   _____

2. Why is the engineer so upset with the timbering in the mines? What does he see as the biggest problem for management?

   _____

   _____

   _____

3. The bourgeois capitalists have certain theories about why the workers cannot become successful. They base their ideas on what they see as a flawed lifestyle. What are their theories?

   _____

   _____

(continued)

4. Why do you think the Grégoires will not give Maheude money when she begs for it?

_____

_____

_____

_____

5. What forms of entertainment do you see at the Montsou fair? How are they similar to, or different from, what you might find at a fair today?

_____

_____

_____

_____

6. How does Souvarine's solution to the problems of the world differ from the solutions offered by Étienne and Rasseneur?

_____

_____

_____

_____

7. Compare the marriage engagement of Zacharie Maheu and Philomène with that of Paul Négrel and Cécile Grégoire. How are they different?

_____

_____

_____

_____

(continued)

8. Why do the soldiers fire upon the miners? Who is to blame for the bloodshed?

_____

_____

_____

_____

9. Why does Souvarine sabotage the mine?

_____

_____

_____

_____

10. At the end of the film, Étienne still has hope that a better world will come. Why is this film (and the novel it is based on) called *Germinal*?

_____

_____

_____

_____

— A TEACHER'S GUIDE TO FEATURE FILMS AND DOCUMENTARY SOURCES —

One common theme taught in world history classes is exploration and expansion. This theme has presented a challenge to every civilization throughout history. Many films use exploration as a subject; a list of such films is provided below, in order of their historical time frame. The Film Analysis Guide Sheet (Appendix A) can be used in the classroom with any of these films. Remember, it is often not necessary to show an entire film to a class. You should feel free to select just certain scenes that serve your educational purposes best.

EXPLORATION BEFORE 1800

Aquirre, The Wrath of God (1978, 90 minutes) This film portrays the 1560 Spanish expedition to explore the Amazon River. The expedition is taken over by a soldier of fortune named Aquirre, who launches his own reign of terror.

Black Robe (1991, 101 minutes) Based on a novel and screenplay by Brian Moore, this film looks at the Jesuits in New France in about 1634. The story focuses on their attempts to convert the natives and to understand the new land in which they have arrived. Rated **R**

Cabeza de Vaca (1991, 120 minutes) This award-winning Spanish film is about the 1528 journey of Alvar Nunez Cabeza de Vaca. When his expedition is destroyed by a storm, de Vaca spends eight years traveling through the American southwest trying to find his comrades.

Christopher Columbus: The Discovery (1992, 120 minutes) This is more of a costume drama than anything else. One of two movies made to celebrate the 500th anniversary of Columbus's voyage, this film concentrates on the period before the voyage. It covers the tribulations that Columbus had to endure before his expedition, including a grilling by the Inquisitor Torquemada (played by Marlon Brando). This film received very poor reviews.

1492: The Conquest of Paradise (1992, 154 minutes) Directed by Ridley Scott, this is probably the better of the two 1992 films about Columbus. This version deals more with the impact of Columbus on the New World. Gérard Depardieu attempts to make Columbus more human and less an iconic figure.

The Mission (1986, 125 minutes) Jeremy Irons and Robert DeNiro star in this film about a Spanish Jesuit who tries to found a mission in early sixteenth-century Brazil.

Seven Cities of Gold (1955, 103 minutes) This film is about the 1769 Spanish expedition to California to find the fabled Seven Cities of Gold and Father Junipero Serra's efforts to build missions and convert the Indians.

The Silk Road (1988, 99 minutes, also known as *Dun-Huang*) Set in eleventh-century China, this Japanese movie involves a romance placed in the context of the Silk Road.

EXPLORATION 1800–1900

Burke and Wills (1985, 141 minutes) This film deals with the tragic 1860–61 expedition to cross Australia from south to north.

Flight of the Eagle (1982, 139 minutes) This Swedish movie tells the story of three foolhardy explorers who try to reach the North Pole in a balloon named the Orient Eagle in 1897.

Forbidden Territory: Stanley's Search for Livingstone (1997, 92 minutes) Shot on location in East Africa, this made-for-television movie tells the story of the 1871 event when Henry Morton Stanley finds the famous explorer-missionary Dr. David Livingstone in what is now Tanzania.

Heart of Darkness (1994, 108 minutes) This made-for-television movie is based on Joseph Conrad's novel of the same name. A trader named Marlow is sent up an African river to discover what has been going on at a trading post deep in the African interior.

Mountains of the Moon (1990, 140 minutes) Based upon William Harrison's book *Burton and Speke,* this film tells the story of English explorers Richard Burton and John Hanning Speke and their rivalry over discovering the source of the White Nile.

POLAR EXPLORATION IN THE TWENTIETH CENTURY

Cook and Peary: The Race to the North Pole (1983, 104 minutes) Based on Frederick Cook's own accounts, this television movie revises the generally accepted version of the conquest of the North Pole.

Glory and Honor (1998, 120 minutes) This television movie gives Robert E. Peary the credit of discovering the Pole in 1909 rather than Frederick Cook. However, it focuses on the role played by Peary's African-American partner (called his "valet" at the time), Matthew Henson.

The Last Place on Earth (1985, 392 minutes) This Masterpiece Theatre series describes the race to the South Pole. Shot in England, Canada, Norway, Scotland, and Greenland, it is based on Roland Huntsford's book *Scott and Amundsen.* The series incorporates the portions of Scott's diaries that were removed by his wife and sponsors after his death.

Shackleton (2002, 300 minutes) This A&E network series dramatizes Ernest Shackleton's 1914 expedition to cross Antarctica via the South Pole. Caught in pack ice before he even gets to the continent, Shackleton (played by Kenneth Branagh) succeeds in saving himself and all 27 men who have accompanied him.

South in the Grip of Black Ice (1919, 88 minutes) A restored documentary, this film uses original footage taken during the Shackleton expedition. It might prove interesting to compare this with the more recent feature film on the same topic.

EXPLORATION IN OUTER SPACE

Apollo 13 (1995, 140 minutes) Directed by Ron Howard, this film portrays the true story of a 1970 mission to the moon during which serious technical problems arose. The movie focuses on how these critical conditions were resolved.

From the Earth to the Moon (1998, 12 episodes, 60 minutes each) This television miniseries was the brainchild of Tom Hanks and inspired by his role in *Apollo 13.* With a huge cast, it portrays America's efforts to reach the moon from the Mercury and Gemini projects to the Apollo project.

Imperialism

TEACHER'S GUIDE

ZULU DAWN

Zulu Dawn Films, 1979; directed by Douglas Hickox, color, 117 minutes

BACKGROUND OF THE FILM

This film is actually the prequel* to the more popular and acclaimed film *Zulu* (1964). Historically, *Zulu Dawn* is better for classroom use because it is less a study in personalities (which *Zulu,* with its star-studded cast, was) and more a study in imperialist attitudes. It also gives a good background to the Zulu Wars, which began in 1879, and shows how the Zulus were able to defeat the technologically superior Europeans.

The Zulus were a Bantu tribe that was turned into a well-disciplined military machine by Shaka, their king, in the early part of the nineteenth century. The political situation in southern Africa then, as now, was unstable. By 1879, the British controlled the Cape Colony and Natal. Land within these territories was disputed between the Boers (descendants of the original Dutch inhabitants of the Cape Colony) and the Zulus under the leadership of a powerful king, Cetshwayo. The British governor, Sir Henry Bartle Frere, viewed Zululand, a large independent native nation in the midst of these states, as a threat to British supremacy. Governor Frere sent a message to Cetshwayo that was virtually an ultimatum: Submit Zululand to British supervision, or British troops

*Prequel is film slang for a movie that is made after another film but covers actions or events that occur before those of the first film. (For instance, Indiana Jones and the Temple of Doom is the prequel to Raiders of the Lost Ark.)

would move into Zululand and take action. This ultimatum was not the policy of the Colonial Secretary in London, but efforts to stop it reached Frere too late. On January 11, 1879, British troops under the command of Lord Chelmsford crossed the border from Natal into Zululand.

Confident of a quick victory due to their modern weaponry, the British were, nonetheless, faced by a formidable opponent. The Zulu nation maintained approximately 50,000 men in its *impis,* or armies. All Zulu males were required to serve from their teens until they were no longer physically capable of fighting. Zulus were highly trained and disciplined. Young warriors were forbidden to marry; they remained in enforced celibacy until they reached the age of 40 or proved themselves in battle. War provided the Zulus a chance to "wash their spears in blood" and escape celibacy.

The tactic used by an *impi* had not changed since Shaka's time. The commander of the *impi* would split his army into four divisions, which would fan out like the horns of a charging buffalo. Two divisions formed the enveloping horns, one unit was the center command, and one unit backed the center as a reserve. Since all that the warriors carried were shields and spears (*assegais*), a Zulu *impi* could move very quickly. There was no other plan or tactic, just a sudden massed assault of great numbers, with no follow-up or exploitation of a victory.

In the Battle of Isandhlwana, pictured in the film, the British suffered a disastrous defeat, losing over 1,700 men. Confronted by the main Zulu *impi* of 20,000, the British with their guns and artillery could

---

not hold out. Although the British eventually did win the Zulu Wars, the invincibility and arrogance of a major European power was seriously shaken by this defeat.

This film accurately portrays the motives and tactics of the British army in entering Zululand. The characters, with the exception of William Vereker, are based on real people. Even the seemingly contrived love interest between Colonel Durnford and the bishop's daughter is based on fact. *Zulu Dawn* was filmed on location in Zululand, with the descendants of the Zulu warriors acting as extras. Have your students note the British attitudes toward the native peoples, but also note that many Europeans expressed outrage at the unjustified invasion of Zululand and expressed humanitarian concerns like those of Bishop Colenso. This film does an excellent job of portraying the events leading up to and during the Battle of Isandlwana and makes an honest attempt to be accurate.

SYNOPSIS OF THE PLOT

At the high commissioner's residence in Pietermaritzburg, Natal, Sir Henry Bartle Frere is reading a dispatch from the British government to Lord Chelmsford, commander of British troops in Natal. The government wants a negotiated settlement with the Zulus; Frere and Chelmsford do not.

The scene switches to a military parade ground where the British troops are being inspected. Native troops are also being trained by British officers, who openly show their contempt toward the natives. Meanwhile at the Zulu village, or *kraal,* a messenger arrives for the king, Cetshwayo. The British make various demands, including one that the king disband his *impis.* Cetshwayo states that he does not go into British territory but that he will defend his land against any who attempt to impose their will on the Zulus.

The scene switches to a lawn party at the commissioner's residence—a slice of Victorian England in Africa. Differing opinions are voiced on how to treat the Zulus. One Briton states that Zulus are raised as

warriors and thus want a war. Bishop Colenso has a different attitude; he feels privileged to share this land with the Zulus. Frere announces that a state of war with the Zulus exists despite the fact that the Zulu king has not crossed into British territory.

Preparations begin for war, and the companies march out. Lord Chelmsford assigns the seasoned soldier Colonel Durnford to defend the Natal border rather than stay with the main force, much to Durnford's anger. At Rorke's Drift, the army crosses the Buffalo River into Zululand. A newspaper correspondent, Norris Newman, questions Chelmsford as to why he is going after the Zulus. Newman believes that the British are attacking for sport and reputation.

King Cetshwayo gathers his people at their *kraal.* He tells them that the British have broken their promise; the Zulus must fight to survive. Meanwhile, Lord Chelmsford has moved his forces deeper into Zululand to Isandhlwana. The British feel confident and infallible. The first to see the forces of the Zulu is a lone trader, who turns tail and runs. He is pursued by three Zulus who allow themselves to be taken prisoner by the British. They give the British false information that the *impis* have moved east. When a Boer volunteer tells Chelmsford to *laager* (circle) his wagons for defense, Chelmsford arrogantly replies that Boers may need to do that, but that the superior British army doesn't.

Colonel Durnford arrives in camp to warn Chelmsford that intelligence sources say the Zulus are moving north to threaten Chelmsford's left. Chelmsford refuses to believe this. He splits his forces, taking half east with him to find the Zulu. Durnford and his troops arrive at Isandhlwana on January 22. The Zulu prisoners escape to warn their king. Meanwhile, Chelmsford's troops are on the road. The newsman questions the wisdom of splitting the forces before the exact location of the enemy is known. Chelmsford's secretary says that this is only a concern when fighting European forces.

At Isandhlwana, Durnford and Lieutenant Vereker take a force to scout for the *impis.* They come across an enormous number of Zulus hidden in a ravine. A messenger is sent to Lord Chelmsford and back to the camp at Isandhlwana. Warned, Colonel Pulleine prepares for battle. The soldiers are precisely lined up and stakes are set out to mark the line of defense. In his camp, Chelmsford sits at an elegant table for luncheon, despite the fact that his soldiers do not have any food to eat.

At Isandhlwana, the Zulus attack. The sophisticated European equipment proves no deterrent to the massive numbers of the *impi*. Due to strict regulations set down by Chelmsford, the ammunition is slow in being handed out, and as the Zulus overrun the camp, the fighting becomes hand-to-hand. The Zulus are victorious in what becomes set down in history as the worst defeat of a modern army by native forces. Chelmsford arrives at night to find the camp silent and burning. It is reported to him that Rorke's Drift is in flames. The film ends with a Zulu *impi* on the move, overlaid by a quote from Benjamin Disraeli: "Who are these Zulus; who are these remarkable people who defeat our generals, convert our bishops, and who on this day have put an end to a great dynasty?" (Interestingly enough, most moviegoers would tend to think this "end to a great dynasty" refers to the decline of British military power, when in reality it refers to the death of the Prince Imperial, the exiled son of Napoléon III, who was killed later on in the Zulu Wars, thus ending the Bonaparte dynasty, albeit in exile, of France.)

IDEAS FOR CLASS DISCUSSION

The motives for European imperialism as expressed in this film could certainly be a good topic for class discussion. What are the motives for war given by both sides? The ways in which the British justify their actions could also be pointed out, because this justification does not apply only to Africa, but to other areas of the world absorbed by the British Empire. The British method of fighting versus that of the Zulus could be discussed, as well as the differences shown between the British officer class and the enlisted men.

BOOKS AND MATERIALS RELATING TO THIS FILM AND TOPIC

Barthorp, Michael. *The Zulu War: A Pictorial History* (Blandford Press, 1980).

Colenso, Frances E. *History of the Zulu War and Its Origin,* reprint of 1880 edition (Negro University Press).

Killingray, David. *A Plague of Europeans* (Penguin Education, 1973).

Knight, Ian. *Isandhlwana 1879: The Great Zulu Victory* (Osprey Press Campaign Series, 2001).

Morris, Donald R. *A Washing of the Spears: The Rise and Fall of the Zulu Nation* (Touchstone Books, 1969).

Wilkinson-Latham, Christopher. *Uniforms and Weapons of the Zulu War* (Hippocrene Books, 1978).

Note—There is an excellent web site devoted to the Zulu Wars and particularly the events of this film: www.rorkesdriftvc.com

OTHER MEDIA RESOURCES FOR THIS TIME PERIOD

Breaker Morant (1979, 107 minutes) Although this film deals with the Boer War, it has a larger theme of individual accountability in time of war.

The Four Feathers (2002, 125 minutes) Based on a 1902 novel, this story has been told in several films. It is the story of cowardice and courage during the British reconquest of the Sudan.

Khartoum (1966, 128 minutes) This film details the siege of Khartoum and its defense by Charles "Chinese" Gordon, which leads to his "martyrdom." Charlton Heston plays Gordon and Laurence Olivier plays his antagonist, the Mahdi.

Lagaan (2002, 225 minutes) Nominated for an Academy Award for the Best Foreign Film, this film focuses on British rule in India. It highlights the efforts of Indian citizens to avoid paying a crippling tax to Britain by winning a game of cricket.

The Last Emperor (1988, 160 minutes) This award-winning film is about Henry Pu Yi, the last Manchu emperor of China and a victim of the forces of history.

Out of Africa (1985, 160 minutes) An award-winning film about white settlement in East Africa, this story concentrates on Danish novelist Karen Blixen.

Shaka Zulu (1983, 300 minutes) This is a controversial made-for-television biography of the early nineteenth-century leader who molded the Zulu warriors into a federation.

Young Winston (1972, 189 minutes) This film about the early life of Winston Churchill covers his imperialistic adventures in Africa, which won him fame and popularity in England.

Zulu (1964, 138 minutes) This film picks up where *Zulu Dawn* leaves off, portraying the successful British defense of the fort at Rorke's Drift.

Imperialism

ZULU DAWN

Zulu Dawn Films, 1979; directed by Douglas Hickox

Major Character	Actor/Actress
General Lord Chelmsford	Peter O'Toole
Colonel Durnford	Burt Lancaster
Sir Henry Bartle Frere	John Mills
Lieutenant William Vereker	Simon Ward
Bishop Colenso	Freddie Jones
King Cetshwayo	Simon Sabela
Colonel Hamilton-Brown	Nigel Davenport
Lt. Colonel Pulleine	Denholm Elliott
Norris-Newman	Ronald Lacey
Colonel Crealock	Michael Jayston

WHAT TO WATCH FOR

This film is a prequel* to the highly acclaimed film *Zulu* (1964). It is a more useful film than *Zulu* in history classes because it gives the background of the British involvement in South Africa and the Zulu War of 1879.

The Zulus were a Bantu tribe that was turned into a highly disciplined war machine by Shaka, their chief from 1818 to 1828. All Zulu males served in the *impi*, or army, from late adolescence to old age. Warriors were not permitted to marry until they were 40 years old or had "washed their spears in blood," either in battle or by brave acts. The king of the Zulus in 1879 was Cetshwayo, who controlled a large independent territory called Zululand.

Prequel is film slang for a movie that is made after another film but covers actions or events that occur before those of the first film. (For instance, *Indiana Jones and the Temple of Doom* is the prequel to *Raiders of the Lost Ark*.)

(continued)

The British by 1879 controlled most of South Africa, including the state of Natal, which bordered Zululand. British officials were concerned by the presence of an independent native state. They also wished to show the Boers—white settlers of Dutch ancestry—that they could control the native peoples. Most historians and many British government officials believed that Lord Chelmsford's invasion of Zululand was not justified. The British did eventually defeat the Zulus, but not before receiving some setbacks to their notion of invincibility and superiority.

Watch for the attitudes expressed in this film by the British. The imperialist concept of European superiority was common in the late nineteenth century. While there were people like Bishop Colenso, the more prevalent attitude was the one conveyed by Lord Chelmsford. Look for examples of prejudice against native peoples and lack of regard for the lives of non-Europeans. Unfortunately, some of these attitudes have carried through to the twentieth century and were displayed during the war in Vietnam. Note the confidence and bravado of the British army. Remember that late nineteenth-century Europeans (and Americans) believed it was their God-given destiny to control the world.

Screening Notes

Imperialism

―――――― *ZULU DAWN* ――――――

VOCABULARY

Bantu   *laager*

Boer   Natal

Cape Colony   Transvaal

impi   Zululand

kraal

QUESTIONS BASED ON THE FILM

1. How are the native people employed by the British army treated by the Europeans?

   _____

   _____

   _____

2. What are the differences in treatment between the British officers and enlisted men?

   _____

   _____

   _____

3. How does King Cetshwayo defend his actions in Zululand when confronted by the British ultimatum?

   _____

   _____

   _____

(continued)

4. As the British troops enter Zululand, what is their justification for the invasion?

_____

_____

_____

_____

5. Why do the British feel confident of victory over the Zulu?

_____

_____

_____

_____

6. Compare the British style of fighting with that of the Zulu. Why are the Zulu victorious at Isandhlwana?

_____

_____

_____

_____

TEACHER'S GUIDE

ALL QUIET ON THE WESTERN FRONT

Universal Pictures, 1930; directed by Lewis Milestone, black and white, 130 minutes

BACKGROUND OF THE FILM

This film, based on the novel of the same title by Erich Maria Remarque, was one of the first to break the romantic cinematic image of war as a glorious spectacle. The book and film, told from the German side, portray World War I as the tragic and terrible waste of life it was. For the production, Universal Pictures built a military camp in California and turned 20 acres into the Western Front, complete with trenches. Over 2,000 ex-servicemen were employed as extras for the battle scenes. The film won Academy Awards for Best Picture and Best Director of 1930. While it was well received in the United States, in Germany there were protests against the film. In Berlin, squads of Nazis let rats and snakes loose in theaters where the film was being shown. Finally, the movie was banned as being a demoralizing influence on youth. Remarque, who fought for Germany in World War I, was exiled and eventually came to the United States. In 1939, this film was rereleased with an anti-Nazi narration by Gordon Kahn.

The technology of twentieth-century warfare and the resulting loss of life are very well demonstrated in this film. The use of the machine gun, heavy artillery, and aerial bombing are portrayed, as well as the conditions of trench warfare. The primitiveness of medical facilities in a time before penicillin and antibiotics is also shown. Amputations were very common, as was shell shock, a mental condition caused by the strain of being under constant bombardment in the trenches. Food shortages caused by the war are demonstrated by the scene with the soldiers and the French girls who are willing to sell themselves for the food that the soldiers bring. The deprivations faced by the soldiers in the trenches were also particularly trying for the Germans, as the British blockaded Germany during the course of the war and prevented supplies from reaching them.

Keep in mind the date of this film when showing it to students. Sound in movies was a relatively new process (1927); today's sophisticated special effects of simulated hellfire and artillery were many years in the future. Most of the actors were used to silent pictures, so their acting tends to be very dramatic. One interesting fact involves the scene with Paul and the French soldier whom he has just bayoneted. The actor playing the Frenchman suffered from a throat disease and could not talk. The advent of talking pictures thus meant the end of his career, except for this one part where speaking was not necessary.

SYNOPSIS OF THE PLOT

This movie can be shown very easily as a series of scenes, since it is not a drama with a complex plot. You can pick and choose scenes depending on your class time constraints. The story concerns Paul Baumer, a German schoolboy, and his friends who join the army at the beginning of the war. The opening scene captures the enthusiasm with which all nations faced World War I. The schoolmaster is encouraging Paul and his friends to enlist, while in the background a military parade can be seen outside. The boys' youthful excitement fades quickly as they go through training under the sadistic command of Himmelstoss, their former postman. In their first experience at the front, they are taught to survive by Sergeant Katczinsky (Kat), a tough veteran. The grim reality of the war is brought home when the first of their classmates (Behm) is killed.

A particularly good scene is one in which the soldiers get enough food because half of the company are casualties, yet the cook has prepared food for the full number. The comrades begin to talk about how a war is started and who benefits by it. The hopelessness of trench warfare is well portrayed; after a long period of fighting and many casualties, the trench positions are the same, with neither side gaining any ground. In one battle scene, Paul kills a French soldier when he jumps into a shell hole where Paul has sought safety. Paul must stay in the hole during the shelling and is filled with remorse. He talks to the dead man, asking forgiveness and promising to care for his family. When the bombardment is over, Paul quickly leaves, and guilt and promises are forgotten.

When Paul goes home on leave, we see that his village is deserted, stores are closed, and a one-legged veteran hobbles down the street. The schoolmaster is still making his patriotic pitch to his young students. Seeing Paul, he asks him to tell the class about the valorous life at the front. Paul's negative response shocks the class.

Paul cuts his leave short and returns to the front, where he finds that most of his comrades have been killed. He seeks out Kat. They reminisce and talk of the future, but Kat is killed by a tiny shell splinter that pierces his skull. In the last scene, Paul is alone in the trenches. He sees a butterfly and reaches for it as a French sniper appears. As we see Paul's hand come closer to the butterfly, we hear a single shot; his hand goes limp. The credits are rolled over a field of crosses as Paul and his dead comrades march away. One by one they turn and look back at the audience, reminding us of the waste of young lives cut short.

IDEAS FOR CLASS DISCUSSION

This film certainly demonstrates the incredible destructive nature of trench warfare and the reasons for the high loss of life during World War I. The contrast between the early optimism and patriotism and the grim realities of war make a good topic for class discussion. The World War I generation has sometimes been called the Lost Generation. How does the film demonstrate this? The scene where the soldiers discuss the motives for the war and how the war got started is particularly telling.

BOOKS AND MATERIALS RELATING TO THIS FILM AND TOPIC

Brownlow, Kevin. *The War, the West, and the Wilderness* (Knopf, 1979).

Isenberg, Michael. *War on Film: The American Cinema and World War I, 1914–1941* (Fairleigh Dickinson University Press, 1981).

Kelly, Andrew. *Filming* All Quiet on the Western Front: *"Brutal Cutting, Stupid Censors, Bigoted Politicos"* (I. B. Taurus, 1998).

Lyons, Timothy. *Hollywood and World War I, Journal of Popular Film, Vol. 1* (Winter 1972, p. 1530).

Zinman, David. *50 Classic Motion Pictures* (Chelsea House, 1983).

OTHER MEDIA RESOURCES FOR THIS TIME PERIOD

Civilization (1916, 102 minutes) Directed by Thomas Ince, this is a classic. It is a lavishly produced plea for universal peace. Its pacifist message was very popular during World War I, when it first came out.

Gallipoli (1981, 111 minutes) Young Australians sign up to join the ANZAC forces and are sent to Gallipoli to participate in Winston Churchill's ill-fated attempt to take Turkey out of World War I.

Oh! What a Lovely War (1969, 139 minutes) Directed by Richard Attenborough, this film graphically displays the change in attitude from enthusiasm to disillusionment with which Europeans, particularly the British, viewed the war.

Paths of Glory (1957, 86 minutes) Stanley Kubrick's film on the futility of war tells about a power-hungry French commander. He orders an impossible attack; when his men mutiny, they are put on trial for cowardice.

Regeneration (1997, 105 minutes) A film based on Pat Barker's novel, it details the story of English poet Siegfried Sassoon and his stay at a mental institution. He was sent there ostensibly for emotional problems, but in reality because he spoke out in opposition to the war. Rated **R**

Wings (1927, 139 minutes) This film, directed by William Wellman, won the first Academy Award given for Best Picture. Its antiwar message tells the story of two friends who join the air corps in World War I.

World War I

ALL QUIET ON THE WESTERN FRONT

Universal Pictures, 1930; directed by Lewis Milestone

Major Character	Actor/Actress
Paul Bäumer	Lew Ayres
Katczinsky (Kat)	Louis Wolheim
Himmelstoss	John Wray
Tjaden	George (Slim) Summerville
Müller	Russell Gleason
Kemmerick	Ben Alexander
Albert	William Bakewell
Kantorek (the schoolmaster)	Arnold Lucy

WHAT TO WATCH FOR

This film won an Academy Award® for Best Picture. It is one of the early sound films; you will notice that the sound quality is inconsistent. The acting is also very dramatic, because most of the actors were used to appearing either on the stage or in silent films. The film shows World War I from the German viewpoint, but it has a universal theme—the wasteful loss of life caused by war. The early scene in the school classroom demonstrates the enthusiasm with which the war was first greeted. Note how the schoolboys' early excitement turns to disillusionment as they go through training under the stern eye of their former postman, Himmelstoss. The full horror sets in when the first of the friends is killed while on a routine wiring mission.

Note the scene when the company has had a hearty meal; the comrades talk about how a war begins and who benefits. The scenes of trench warfare are also quite accurate. Over 2,000 ex-soldiers were employed as extras. Note how twentieth-century technology turns this into a war of attrition. Neither side can move forward

(continued)

without an incredible loss of life. Shell shock (a mental condition caused by the stress of constant bombardment and the threat of death) was very common among soldiers during this war. Note the primitive conditions in the military field hospitals. Remember that this takes place before penicillin and antibiotics have been invented. Amputation was the common remedy for a wound to the limbs. Be certain to compare Paul's hometown as it is pictured when he goes home on leave with what it is like in the opening scenes of the movie. Germany was blockaded by the British navy during the war. Although civilian populations suffered in every country that was involved (note the French girls who are desperate for food), German citizens had serious shortages of food, fuel, and other essentials.

Screening Notes

—— ALL QUIET ON THE WESTERN FRONT ——

VOCABULARY

armistice

artillery

attrition

barbed wire

grenade

Kaiser

shell shock

trench warfare

Western Front

QUESTIONS BASED ON THE FILM

1. What is the attitude of the boys and their schoolmaster at the beginning of the film? How do they view the war?

_____

_____

_____

_____

2. When do the boys first realize that training for the army may not be as glorious as they have imagined?

_____

_____

_____

_____

(continued)

3. What happens to Franz Kemmerick? What is the attitude of his friends when they come to visit him at the hospital?

_____

_____

_____

_____

4. Why is there so much extra food in the scene where the cooks prepare a meal? How do the soldiers decide that a disagreement should be settled so as to avoid a war?

_____

_____

_____

_____

5. Comment on the destruction to civilian property and the effect on civilians in the war zone. Why was trench warfare so destructive?

_____

_____

_____

_____

6. How does Paul's attitude toward the French soldier he has killed change once the shelling is over?

_____

_____

_____

(continued)

7. How has Paul's village changed since he left for the front? Has the schoolmaster changed his attitude?

_____

_____

_____

_____

8. How have things changed for the Germans since Paul left his comrades after being wounded?

_____

_____

_____

_____

9. The men who fought in World War I have sometimes been referred to as the Lost Generation. Considering the film, why do you think that this is so?

_____

_____

_____

_____

The Russian Revolution

TEACHER'S GUIDE

NICHOLAS AND ALEXANDRA

Horizon Pictures, 1971; directed by Franklin J. Schaffner, color, 183 minutes

BACKGROUND OF THE FILM

This film is based on the best-selling book of the same title by Robert K. Massie. Massie became interested in the Russian royal family upon learning that his son had hemophilia, the same disease the tsarevich had. Using many primary source materials, Massie came to the conclusion voiced by Alexander Kerensky—that without Rasputin, there could have been no Lenin, and that the tsarevich's illness and the parents' response to it were the cause of the Romanovs' downfall. The film, like the book, thus concentrates on the personalities of the royal couple, often to the exclusion of the wider political issues of the time.

Nicholas is accurately portrayed as weak and vacillating, unintelligent and stubborn, henpecked and wholly dependent upon his wife. This portrait is verified by the couple's personal letters, some of which contribute to the dialogue in the film. Alexandra is portrayed, perhaps, as too sane. Her fanatic devotion to Rasputin and her intransigent belief in autocracy made the tsarina a figure of even more scorn and distrust than is shown in the film, which makes her somewhat more pitiable than she really was.

The problem with this film from a historical standpoint is its tendency to make Nicholas and Alexandra into tragic figures—portraying them more as people caught up in the events of history than as the causers of these events. We are told that the Romanovs have brought untold misery to the people, but we only catch fleeting glimpses of the wretched conditions of the majority of Russians, such as the scene in the Putilov factory in 1905 or the peasants watching the drunken celebration of the Romanovs' tercentenary in 1913. The film thus takes a fundamentally biographical approach that concentrates on the personal tragedies of one family and diminishes the atrocities committed against the untold millions. The revolutionaries are presented as wild-eyed, power-hungry fanatics, not worthy objects of our sympathy or understanding.

This film has some merit as a vehicle for history classes. The opulence, decadence, and isolation of the Russian elite are carefully portrayed in sumptuous costumes and sets. Also, some portrayals do hit the mark very well historically: Count Witte counseling moderation for the unprepared Russia at the outset of the war, the blustering overconfidence of the tsar's officers and reference to the "pansy-Kaiser," the Allied pressure on the provisional government to stay in the war, and the irresolution at Ekaterinburg. The scene with Nicholas returning to his palace after abdication is not only poignant but also accurate. Synopsizing an event as complex as the Russian Revolution is, of course, a problem. Historical inaccuracies do appear, such as having Kerensky act as the head of the government in April when Lenin returned to Russia.

If you can put "Nicky," "Sunny," and their tragedy in proper perspective, this film can serve well in discussion and study of the Russian Revolution and the events leading to it.

SYNOPSIS OF THE PLOT

The film opens with the birth of the long-awaited son and heir to the throne. At the royal estate, Nicholas must meet with Count Witte. Alexandra urges him to be firm; as tsar, everyone is his servant. Russia is involved in a war with Japan. Witte warns the tsar that the people want reforms and that the war is disastrous. Nicholas is unmoved.

Nicholas and Alexandra attend the dowager empress's birthday party. Rasputin arrives at the party and is introduced as a *starets,* a holy man with the power of healing. Later, the royal couple is told that the tsarevich has hemophilia and that the tsarina is the carrier. While Nicholas and Alexandra are in St. Petersburg blessing the troops, they receive the message that their son is bleeding. Rasputin is sent for, and Alexandra prays with him.

In the wave of unrest during the 1905 war with Japan, a young priest, Father Gapon, leads the factory workers on a peaceful march to petition the tsar. The tsar's soldiers fire into the crowd, killing many.

At their Crimean estate, the royal family is relaxing. Count Stolypin visits the tsar to make him aware of vile rumors about the relationship between Rasputin and Alexandra. Back in St. Petersburg, Nicholas forces Rasputin to leave the city. Meanwhile, the Russian revolutionaries in exile in Switzerland are plagued by spies from the tsar's secret police, the *okhrana.* Lenin bemoans his fate as an émigré.

The tsar is celebrating 300 years of Romanov rule at the opera when Stolypin is assassinated. The tsar demands retribution, and the Duma is suspended. A young man named Kerensky protests vehemently.

At the royal hunting lodge in Poland, the tsarevich, Alexei, injures himself. He begins to hemorrhage and is near death. Alexandra writes to Rasputin and receives a response that the tsarevich will not die. Alexei recovers, and Rasputin once more is accepted as part of the royal household.

After the assassination at Sarajevo, Nicholas orders a mobilization against Austria. The Russian generals hope for war and enthusiastically support the mobilization. There is united support at the beginning of the war. As the war goes poorly, Nicholas is determined to go to the front and take personal command himself, despite the opposition of his ministers. Conditions in the army are desperate as Nicholas arrives to take command from his uncle, the Grand Duke Nicholas.

Meanwhile, in St. Petersburg, Rasputin peddles his influence. He is invited to Prince Yusupov's house for an evening of debauchery. Rasputin is fed cyanide poison but doesn't die. He is shot but staggers out of the house. Finally, Rasputin is beaten and killed. Alexandra is hysterical and refuses to meet with government ministers. The situation in St. Petersburg is critical—there is no food and no fuel. When soldiers are sent out to stop the bread riots, they join the people. The tsar is notified of conditions but refuses to return to the city. In his railroad car, Nicholas is told that the Duma has taken over and has ordered his abdication. Without the support of his generals, Nicholas is forced to give up the throne.

Nicholas arrives at his palace to find it overrun with soldiers. He is reunited with Alexandra in an emotional scene. At the royal estate, the tsar and his family plant vegetables. The tsar is summoned by Alexander Kerensky, who tells him that his government is pledged to the war and that the royal family is being moved to Siberia.

Lenin arrives in St. Petersburg and is greeted by enthusiastic crowds. Eventually, the Bolsheviks make their move. They take over all of the major utilities and, finally, the government itself.

In Siberia, the tsar's family is still protected by the now-defunct provisional government. Soldiers from Moscow arrive to take charge of the tsar and his family and move them to a so-called "safe location." They are taken by the Ural Soviet to Ekaterinburg, where they are held in close security. One night, the tsar and his family are told that they are leaving. They are put in a room to wait; soldiers enter, and the entire family is shot to death.

IDEAS FOR CLASS DISCUSSION

A good topic for class discussion would be the complexity of issues surrounding an event of such historical magnitude as the Russian Revolution. Could just one or two persons be responsible, or was it a combination of many different forces operating at the same time? The vast differences in the Russian social classes and the remoteness of the tsarist government from the majority of the people should also be discussed. An interesting side note is that, due to modern forensic science, the remains of the tsar and his family have been identified. The tsar's remains have been placed in the Cathedral of the Fortress of St. Peter and St. Paul, where all of the other tsars are buried. That this event should have occurred certainly tells us something about the change in attitude in Russia after the breakup of the Soviet Union.

BOOKS AND MATERIALS RELATING TO THIS FILM AND TOPIC

Halliday, E. M. *Russia in Revolution* (Harper & Row, 1967).

Massie, Robert K. *Nicholas and Alexandra* (Atheneum, 1967).

Salisbury, Harrison. *Black Night, White Snow: Russia's Revolutions 1905–1917* (Doubleday, 1978).

Vogt, George. *Nicholas II* (Chelsea House Publishers, 1987).

OTHER MEDIA RESOURCES FOR THIS TIME PERIOD

The Battleship Potemkin (1927, Russian, silent, 70 minutes) Sergei Eisenstein's film classic is about the 1905 Revolution.

Dr. Zhivago (1965, 193 minutes) Directed by David Lean, this epic film is based on Boris Pasternak's 1957 novel, which was banned in the Soviet Union.

Reds (1981, 200 minutes) Warren Beatty's film about radical American newspaperman John Reed details Reed's experiences in Russia during the Revolution.

Ten Days That Shook the World (1928, Russian, silent, 102 minutes) Sergei Eisenstein's film about the Bolshevik Revolution was made with the blessing of the Soviet regime.

The Russian Revolution

NICHOLAS AND ALEXANDRA

Horizon Pictures, 1971; directed by Franklin J. Schaffner

Major Character	Actor/Actress
Nicholas	Michael Jayston
Alexandra	Janet Suzman
Grand Duke Nicholas	Harry Andrews
Dowager Empress Marie	Irene Worth
Rasputin	Tom Baker
Count Fredericks	Jack Hawkins
Count Witte	Laurence Olivier
Stolypin	Eric Porter
Sazonov	Michael Redgrave
Kerensky	John McEnery
Lenin	Michael Bryant
Mme. Krupskaya	Vivian Pickles
Trotsky	Brian Cox
Stalin	James Hazeldine

WHAT TO WATCH FOR

This film is based on Robert K. Massie's best-selling book of the same name. Massie first became interested in the Russian royal family when he learned that his son had hemophilia, sometimes known as "bleeder's disease." The heir to the Russian throne, the tsarevich Alexei, also had hemophilia. Since most of the royal families of Europe were related by marriage, the theory is that Queen Victoria was probably the carrier of this disease. The film concentrates on the personalities and personal problems of the Romanov family, particularly Tsar Nicholas and his wife, Alexandra. The portrayals of these historical figures are accurate, even using dialogue taken

(continued)

from their letters. Look for examples of Nicholas's lack of ability as a ruler. When his father died, Nicholas was heard to say, "What is going to happen to me . . . to all of Russia? I am not prepared to be a tsar." Watch also for his unshaken belief in God-given autocracy (unlimited power). Alexandra, a German princess and granddaughter of Queen Victoria, was not popular with the Russian people. Notice how this is shown in the film.

The opulence and decadence of the Russian nobility are well portrayed through the costumes and sets. The wretched conditions of the majority of the Russian people, before and during World War I, are not shown clearly enough. We catch only brief glimpses of the general misery and oppression. Notice turning points when Nicholas could have changed the course of events, when he could have stopped the oncoming revolution and bloodshed. While watching this film, remember to keep your perspective. Remain aware that this film concentrates on the very minor tragedy of the Romanov family as compared with the sufferings of untold millions.

Screening Notes

The Russian Revolution

— *NICHOLAS AND ALEXANDRA* —

VOCABULARY

Bloody Sunday

Bolsheviks

Duma

hemophilia

okhrana

provisional government

Russo-Japanese War

St. Petersburg

Siberia

starets

tsar (czar)

QUESTIONS BASED ON THE FILM

1. Why won't Nicholas end the war with Japan?

   _____

   _____

   _____

2. In the film, the dowager empress states that Russia is an eighteenth-century country in a twentieth-century world. How is this statement true?

   _____

   _____

   _____

3. Bloody Sunday has been called the turning point in the people's attitudes toward the tsar. How is this portrayed in the film?

   _____

   _____

   _____

(continued)

4. Alexandra, according to many historians, was an unstable, hysterical woman who very much affected the tsar's ability to rule. How does the film represent this?

_____

_____

_____

5. What is the attitude of the people of all European nations at the beginning of the war?

_____

_____

_____

6. Why is Rasputin killed?

_____

_____

_____

7. What problems beset Kerensky and his provisional government?

_____

_____

_____

8. How do the Allies put pressure on Kerensky's government to stay in the war?

_____

_____

_____

9. Why are the tsar and his family executed?

_____

_____

_____

— TEACHER'S GUIDE —

GANDHI

Columbia Pictures, 1982; directed by Richard Attenborough, color, 188 minutes. *Gandhi* won eight Academy Awards, including the Oscar for Best Picture.

BACKGROUND OF THE FILM

Mohandas K. Gandhi, known as Mahatma, or the Enlightened One, is one of those charismatic figures of twentieth-century history. He is apt to be the topic of an essay or discussion on "Does the man make history or history make the man?" Richard Attenborough first became interested in making a film about Gandhi in 1962, when he was a well-known actor but had not yet directed a movie. Attenborough was approached by an Indian diplomat living in London, Motilal Kothari. He was encouraged to read the Louis Fischer biography of Gandhi, find a scriptwriter, and ultimately produce and direct a film based on Gandhi's life. Attenborough spent 20 years trying to bring this film to actuality. He spent so much of his own money that he was often on the verge of bankruptcy; he was at times ridiculed for his obsession with this project. Old friendships, such as that with producer Joseph E. Levine, were broken, but Attenborough also made new friends with such luminaries as Pandit Nehru, Indira Gandhi, and Lord Mountbatten. The dedication of Attenborough to this project is demonstrated in the title on the credits, which reads, "Richard Attenborough's film *Gandhi*."

Most of the movie was filmed on location in India. Many of the major figures who knew Gandhi were consulted to add to the accuracy of the film. After much work on Attenborough's part, the Indian Ministry of Information and Broadcasting approved the film. It even participated financially in its production, provided that the film was a joint venture between Attenborough's crew and an Indian company.

This is a very long film, but it is very episodic. Individual segments can be used very effectively. The early sections of the film concerning Gandhi's activities in South Africa are particularly relevant. Although Gandhi was successful in alleviating the discrimination against Indians in South Africa, such as the Pass Laws, he did not change the status of black Africans in South Africa. This is certainly a topic of current concern, even with the changes in the South African government.

SYNOPSIS OF THE PLOT

The film opens with a disclaimer stating that it is impossible to encompass a person's life in one telling, but that rather it is better to try to be faithful to the person's spirit. The scene then opens on New Delhi, India, in January 30, 1948, and shows the assassination of Gandhi. Next the story cuts to South Africa in 1893. Gandhi, a young lawyer, is thrown off a train because he refuses to leave a first-class compartment that he is told Indians cannot occupy. Gandhi decides to fight the discrimination against Indians by holding a peaceful protest, where he burns pass cards despite a beating by the police. The European and American press support Gandhi's actions, and he makes a friend of Charlie Andrews, an Anglican minister. At a meeting of Indians in South Africa to protest new, stricter pass-card regulations, Gandhi sets out his policy of peaceful resistance. Gandhi is thrown into prison for defying the South African government, as are thousands of Indian workers, thus crippling the economy. Gandhi is eventually brought before Prime Minister Smuts and told that the new laws will be repealed. Gandhi and all Indian prisoners will be released.

In 1914, Gandhi returns to India, where he is met by a huge crowd. Hindu and Muslim leaders meet with Gandhi to exhort him to work for home rule. Gandhi takes time to travel around India to discover his country.

When World War I is over, the Indians hold a National Congress party meeting to demand home rule. Gandhi urges the Congress to remember the millions who toil and look for independence as a united nation. At his ashram, Gandhi meets a starving indigo farmer, who tells of his hard life. Gandhi travels to Champara to see conditions firsthand. He attracts a large crowd and is placed under arrest, tried, and eventually ordered out of the province. Gandhi's success in uniting the peasants surprises the government. The landlords make concessions, but new restrictions are placed against Indian resistance. Gandhi calls for a day of prayer and fasting on the day the measures go into effect. The viceroy is notified of this general strike and orders Gandhi's imprisonment. At a peaceful gathering at Amritsar, General Dyer sends in troops. They fire into the unarmed crowd, causing 1,516 casualties.

Gandhi and other Indian leaders meet with the viceroy to discuss reconciliation. Gandhi insists on self-rule. He goes to the people with his message of unity and defiance of British rule. Despite Gandhi's pleas for nonviolence, in Chauri Chaura an Indian crowd storms a police station, and 22 policemen are killed. In response, Gandhi undertakes a fast as penance for the violence. As peace returns and Gandhi ends his fast, he is arrested by the British for sedition. When Gandhi is brought before Judge Broomfield, it is the judge who rises respectfully before the prisoner. Gandhi is sentenced to six years in prison.

Six years later, Gandhi is visited in his home province by William Walker, an American journalist who had known him in South Africa. Gandhi decides that his new act of defiance will be to make salt, a product monopolized by the British. Gandhi walks the 240 miles to the sea and is greeted by large crowds along the way. Hundreds of thousands are arrested for engaging in the illegal salt trade, and finally Gandhi himself is put in jail. Gandhi's followers march against the British-owned Dharasana salt works. They are beaten by the soldiers but show no violence against their attackers.

Gandhi is summoned to New Delhi to meet with the viceroy. He is invited to an all-Indian congress in London about possible Indian independence. In England, Gandhi meets with many English leaders, but the congress comes to naught. Gandhi still believes that independence will come. He states that he will not take advantage of the British being at war with Germany. Gandhi is put in prison for the duration of the war. He is visited by *Life* photojournalist Margaret Bourke-White. While Gandhi is in prison, his wife, Kasturba, dies.

At the war's end, a new viceroy, Lord Mountbatten, takes over to supervise Indian independence. As the time for independence draws near, a split widens between the Muslims and Hindus. The Muslim leader, Jinnah, wants a separate state of Pakistan for Muslims.

Independence is proclaimed, and India is split into two nations. Gandhi does not celebrate. At the India-Pakistan border in August 1947, bloodshed between Muslims and Hindus occurs. Conflict spreads throughout India. Gandhi begins another fast to protest the violence. This time, he is close to death. Nehru does all he can to persuade Gandhi to end his fast.

As order is finally restored, Gandhi ends his fast. The movie ends with Gandhi's assassination, his funeral pyre, and the scattering of his ashes in the sea.

IDEAS FOR CLASS DISCUSSION

The scenes demonstrating Gandhi's policy of nonviolent, passive resistance to achieve a goal would be excellent discussion points. This type of resistance as a means to exact change could also be compared with the U.S. civil rights movement of the 1950s–60s or the Vietnam War protests. Although most of Gandhi's life covers the era before World War II, his ideals and legacy are still felt today. Also, the resistance of many European nations to dissolve their imperialistic ties with their colonies would be a good topic to explore. Were their motives economic or based more on an anachronistic sense of national mission and world power?

BOOKS AND MATERIALS RELATING TO THIS FILM AND TOPIC

Attenborough, Richard. *In Search of Gandhi* (New Century Publishers, 1982).

Cross, Cohn. *The Fall of the British Empire, 1918–1968* (Coward-McCann, 1968).

Fischer, Louis. *The Life of Mahatma Gandhi* (Collier Books, 1950).

Gandhi, Mohandas K. *Autobiography: The Story of My Experiments with Truth* (Beacon Press, 1957).

Moon, Penderel. *Gandhi and Modern India* (W. W. Norton, 1969).

OTHER MEDIA RESOURCES FOR THIS TIME PERIOD

Alexander Nevsky (1938, 105 minutes) Ostensibly about a thirteenth-century Russian hero, this film is really a Soviet warning against German aggression.

Butterfly (2001, 94 minutes) The story of a young boy and his family is set against the background of the Spanish Civil War. Rated **R**

Cabaret (1972, 123 minutes) Winner of eight Academy Awards, this musical is based on Christopher Isherwood's book about Weimar Germany at the beginning of the Nazis' rise to power.

Grand Illusion (1937, 111 minutes) Set in a German POW camp during World War I, this Jean Renoir film explores the relationship between reality and illusion as French captives and their German captors face the facts of their situation. This film is often taken to be a reflection of the disillusionment that sapped French resolve as World War II approached.

The Jewel in the Crown (1984, 750 minutes) Based on Paul Scott's *Raj Quartet,* this PBS series depicts Britain's last years (1942–1947) in India.

Land and Freedom (1995, 109 minutes) A young unemployed communist leaves his native Liverpool in 1936 to fight the fascists in the Spanish Civil War.

A Passage to India (1984, 163 minutes) Based on E. M. Forster's 1924 novel and nominated for 11 Academy Awards, the film deals with an Englishwoman traveling in India in the early twentieth century and the lack of understanding between the native Indians and their British overlords.

White Mischief (1987, 107 minutes) This murder mystery is set among the British living in Kenya at the beginning of World War II. Rated **R**

GANDHI

Columbia Pictures, 1982; directed by Richard Attenborough. *Gandhi* won Academy Awards® for Best Picture, Best Actor (Ben Kingsley), and Best Director.

Major Character	Actor/Actress
Mohandas Gandhi	Ben Kingsley
Kasturba Gandhi	Rohini Hattangady
Margaret Bourke-White	Candice Bergen
General Dyer	Edward Fox
Lord Irwin	John Gielgud
Judge Broomfield	Trevor Howard
The Viceroy	John Mills
William Walker	Martin Sheen
Charlie Andrews	Ian Charleson
Mirabehn	Geraldine James
General Smuts	Athol Fugard
Herman Kallenbach	Günther Maria Halmer
Pandit Nehru	Roshan Seth
Sardar Patel	Saeed Jaffrey
Mohammed Ali Jinnah	Alyque Padansee
Kahn	Amrish Puri

WHAT TO WATCH FOR

Director Richard Attenborough spent 20 years trying to make this film about Indian leader Mohandas Gandhi. Gandhi, also known as Mahatma, the Enlightened One, helped to unify much of India in a campaign of resistance to British rule. The technique Gandhi used and preached about was nonviolent, passive resistance.

(continued)

Watch for examples of this in the film, such as breaking the British economic monopoly in India or protesting unjust laws in South Africa.

The movie was filmed on location in India, and many of the major figures who knew Gandhi were consulted. Remember, though, that this film is not, and could not be, an all-inclusive look at Gandhi's life and times. Note the disclaimer at the beginning of the film. It states that this film attempts to capture the *spirit* of the man; much must be left out due to time contraints.

Gandhi clearly portrays the world after World War I and the end of European domination. Gandhi was a person brought up under imperialism who worked to break that system. He became one of the first non-Europeans to be recognized as a worldwide leader.

Screening Notes

—————— *GANDHI* ——————

VOCABULARY

ashram

Hindu

Mahatma

Mohammed Ali Jinnah

Muslim

Pakistan

Pandit Nehru

passive resistance

untouchables

viceroy

QUESTIONS BASED ON THE FILM

1. On the ashram (commune) in South Africa, what causes the disagreement between Gandhi and his wife?

   _____

   _____

2. What examples in the film show Gandhi's sense of honor and fairness, which earn him the title of Mahatma?

   _____

   _____

   _____

3. How does Gandhi get young, educated Indians involved in his movement?

   _____

   _____

   _____

(continued)

4. What means does Gandhi use to resist British rule in India?

_____

_____

_____

5. Gandhi's spinning wheel is part of the flag of India. What is its significance in the quest for Indian independence?

_____

_____

_____

_____

6. As Indian independence draws near, what problem is facing Gandhi and the Indian leadership?

_____

_____

_____

_____

7. At what other times in history has Gandhi's principle of passive resistance been used?

_____

_____

_____

TEACHER'S GUIDE

CONSPIRACY

HBO Films, 2001; directed by Frank Pierson, color, 96 minutes; rated **R**

BACKGROUND OF THE FILM

Conspiracy presents a case study in what political scientist Hannah Arendt has called "the banality of evil." The Wannsee Conference brought together a group of 15 German government ministerial representatives (several of whom appear on the student reproducible page as Major Characters, labeled with the number 1), conquered Eastern Zone administrators (labeled 2), SS and Nazi party functionaries (3), and security officials (4). These were mostly well educated and competent bureaucrats with special responsibilities for the so-called "Jewish Question." Initially called together in December 1941 by SS General Heydrich, and then postponed until early 1942, the group met on Tuesday, January 20, 1942, at a Security Service (SD) guesthouse at 56-58 Am Grossen Wannsee in a suburb of Berlin. (The house was donated to an SD charitable foundation by a right-wing industrialist hoping to avoid imprisonment for fraud.) The purpose of the conference was to discuss, prioritize, and coordinate a final solution to the "Jewish Question." Though notes were taken at the meeting, organizers went to great lengths to ensure that no transcript of the discussions would remain in existence. Immediately after the war, conference participants denied that it had ever taken place. A single copy of the "Wannsee Protocol" that SS Colonel Eichmann produced after the meeting was discovered by American investigators in the files of

the German Foreign Ministry in 1947. This one copy, along with some self-serving testimony from conference participants trying to absolve themselves of responsibility for the Holocaust in the war-crimes trials that followed, are the only extant accounts of the discussions leading to the Protocol. The dialogue of this film (like that of its [West] German predecessor, *Wannseekonferenz [Wannsee Conference])** is therefore a hypothetical reconstruction of what *could* have been said by the participants based on what is known they knew at the time, on the language of the Protocol itself, and on the actions that were taken in the wake of the conference.

Though the conference has been often referred to as the smoking gun, proving the murderous intent of the Nazi regime toward the Jews, historians themselves do not agree on the purpose or significance of the conference and its resulting Protocol. Some historians, characterized as "intentionalists," believe that the Nazis had always intended to murder the Jewish population of occupied Europe and that Wannsee represented the final operationalization of that policy. Others, called "functionalists," argue that though the Nazis always intended to rid German territory of "impure racial elements," of whom the Jews were the primary example, the Final Solution emerged gradually as other removal methods were foreclosed by both diplomacy and war. Initially, they argue, the Nazis sought to exclude Jews from German citizenship, isolate them, and encourage them to emigrate.

*1984, directed by Heinz Schirk, in German with English subtitles

But worldwide depression and the restrictive immigration policies of other nations (particularly the United States, but also Britain and France, who were unwilling to permit the use of their colonies in the Middle East or Africa as "dumping grounds") made this difficult to achieve. When war broke out in September 1939 and Germany had some early victories, followed by its attack on the Soviet Union in June 1941, the possibility arose that Jews might be deported to territories in the east as a solution to the problem. However, when the Russian war ground to a halt by the winter of 1941 (symbolized by the death, from natural causes, of Army Group South commander Field Marshal Walter von Reichenau), the manpower and food resources hoped for from a quick victory were not available. There were now millions of additional people to feed in the occupied zones. Moreover, whatever advantage the Nazis had hoped to achieve by holding the Jews hostage to continued U.S. neutrality (the Nazis believed that the Roosevelt administration was dominated by Jewish influence), weakened as a motive with the growing American covert support for Britain. (The Lend Lease Act and convoying were two of the strongest indications that such a strategy would not remain effective.) Finally, the American response to the attack on Pearl Harbor in December 1941 prompted the German declaration of war that followed. Faced with these new realities, such historians argue, beginning in July 1941, Nazi policy rapidly evolved from random violence and mass murder to one of evacuation, a code word for annihilation.* Nazi Party ideologue Alfred Rosenberg, at a meeting with Himmler, called it the "biological eradication of the entire Jewry of Europe." For functionalist historians, Wannsee was the point at which the policy of extermination was formalized for the bureaucrats who would have to

carry it out. Both of these views—intentionalist and functionalist—are represented in the film. (The full text of the Protocol appears in Appendix B at the back of this book to facilitate discussion of these issues, as well as of the film's faithfulness to the textual evidence.)

There were other reasons for the Wannsee meeting as well. The SS was interested in asserting its power over the government ministries, party officials, and eastern occupying authorities, especially on matters of race. The tangled web of definitions of "racial purity" and "Jewishness" within greater Germany, based on the 1935 Nuremberg Laws, needed to be sorted out. The fates of exempted Jews (those who were war heroes, had essential skills, or were otherwise "protected"), Jews in mixed marriages (the Nazis estimated that there were some 20,000 in this category) or *Mischlinge* (Germans with one German and one Jewish parent or ancestor)** needed to be defined without causing an uproar among their German relatives. Long discussions about the effectiveness of mass sterilization and the use of "old age" (a euphemism for transit camps like Theresienstadt, or Terezin, in Czechoslovakia) took place at the meeting.*** The growing danger of epidemic and famine in the Polish ghettos, now bursting at the seams with refugees from all over the eastern occupied zones, had to be addressed as well. Finally, faced with exploding war-related demands for manpower, matériel, and transportation resources, the German government was forced to calculate the extent to which deportees could be used to meet the labor demands of the war. It also felt compelled to

---

*This policy is reflected in Reichsmarschall Hermann Göring's post-*Kristalnacht* order to the SS, quoted by Heydrich in the film, to make "all necessary preparations in regard to organizational and technical matters for bringing about a complete solution of the Jewish question in the German sphere of influence in Europe."

**People with one German and one Jewish parent were categorized as First Degree Jews; there were some 64,000 in Germany at the time. People with one German parent and one Jewish ancestor were categorized as Second Degree; there were about 43,000 of these.

***This camp was later made infamous by the German propaganda film made at the time of a Danish Red Cross visit, after which some 88,162 inmates were transported to their deaths as part of Operation Reinhard, named in Heydrich's honor.

prioritize the order of the zones to be made *Judenfrei* ("free of Jews"); Bohemia and Germany went first. All of these matters appear in the Protocol and are discussed in the film.

There is some doubt that the methods of extermination were actually discussed in detail at the meeting. However, the film's writer, Loring Mandel, has its participants articulate what many of them knew (or should have known at that point) about the euthanasia (T-4) program. Undertaken by Nazi doctors before the outbreak of the war to rid the country of handicapped and mentally ill Germans ("life unworthy of life"), the program was forced underground by outraged German public opinion when it was exposed. The conference attendees also knew about the mass shootings by SS *Einsatzgruppen* ("operations units") in the south and east and the psychological effects on the perpetrators themselves. In addition, they knew about the systematic use of mass starvation as a means of population control, the experiments with mass surgical and X ray-based sterilization, and with electrocution. Mandel has Eichmann reveal to the attendees information about tests with mobile killing vans into which carbon monoxide exhaust fumes were diverted, model fixed gas chambers (constructed by Operation Reinhard) ready for operation,* and the construction of the industrialized extermination and slave-labor facilities at Auschwitz-Birkenau.

*These were implemented beginning in March 1942 at Belzec, Sobibor, and Treblinka concentration camps.

SYNOPSIS OF THE PLOT

After a prologue narration that sets the conference in the context of the Second World War and the Russian campaign, the film shows Heydrich flying his own plane to the meeting. Meanwhile, Eichmann is making sure that everything is perfect at the villa. Officials arrive, beginning with those from occupied Poland (Bühler, Schöngarth, and Lange). As the guests arrive, we witness their interpersonal maneuvers and overhear some of their concerns about the meeting to come. Heydrich arrives, and the meeting convenes with each participant introducing himself. After declaring that "this meeting is not taking place," Heydrich sets forth the meeting's purpose and indicates statistically the magnitude of the "Jewish Question" to be resolved. With the Russian war at a temporary standstill, the United States now in the war, and the ongoing drain on Germany's resources, he says, "we can no longer store Jews." Emigration, he says, is over—what now? "Evacuation" is the new policy, but everyone understands that this is code; they discuss why coyness is being used to avoid the real meaning of the word, annihilation. Luther, representing the Foreign Ministry, reports on the probable reactions from Scandinavia and Italy. Kritzinger protests that the Reichschancellery has previously received assurances from Hitler that annihilation is not the official policy with regard to German Jews.

The discussion then turns to the definition of Jews and to the fate of half- and quarter-Jews, Jews married to Germans, and Jews exempted by the Nuremberg Laws for reasons of state service or occupation. Heydrich offers his conclusions, involving sterilization as an alternative to evacuation, or ghettoization. Kritzinger again protests that Hitler has given assurances, but Heydrich presses forward. There will be no more blanket exemptions; in all cases, the SS will decide. Some around the table call for even more radical solutions. Eichmann outlines the methods used thus far (sterilization, euthanasia, carbon monoxide) to solve the problem. He suggests that "death is the most reliable form of sterilization." Stuckart, the coauthor of the Nuremberg Laws and the representative of the Justice Ministry, calls on his colleagues to drop the gross caricatures of Jewish beastliness and adopt more sophisticated anti-Semitic and racial views. He is attacked as a Jew lover by Klopfer, and an argument ensues.

At lunch, Heydrich warns Stuckart that he risks his career and more by opposing the SS in this matter. (Foreshadowing the fate of the 1944 plotters against Hitler, Heydrich tells Stuckart, "There are [sic] no shortage of meat hooks on which to hang enemies of the state.") Neumann questions the economic consequences of ending the policy of exempting Jews for labor purposes. He is told that, although the two purposes might not be mutually exclusive, the evacuation policy will be paramount. The *Generalgouvernement* representatives again protest that there is no additional capacity to receive refugees in the Polish ghettos until the ghettos themselves are evacuated. There is a growing risk of epidemic spreading to the general population, and even to the German soldiers. Lange is taken aside by Heydrich and reassured. At the same time, Klopfer confides to Müller that Heydrich is rumored to have Jewish blood; Müller suggests that he confront Heydrich with the claim.

When the meeting reconvenes, referring to Stuckart, Heydrich invokes the *Führerprinzip*, reminding the group, "our Führer enunciates the goal; it is our task to turn his vision into reality; we can debate the 'when,' we can debate the 'how,' up to a point, but we cannot debate the 'if.'" Stuckart says that he is only requesting that the process operate within a legal framework; Kritzinger defends his position. A brief discussion ensues about how the Catholic church and the Vatican (as well as the Lutheran church) might respond to the dissolution of mixed marriages; Luther dismisses the concern.

An extended discussion about methods begins. Eichmann recounts the successive methods employed to rid "greater Germany" of Jews. Bühler is surprised by the experimentation taking place under his nose. Hoffmann sickens, but blames his squeamishness on the cigar smoke. Eichmann retreats into the kitchen for whiskey and a bromide. Lange tells Kritzinger about the murder of German Jews in Riga by civilian mobs and his own troops and about rumors of gas chambers. When Kritzinger worries about the legal implications, Lange informs him that he, too, has studied the law, but that it has made him "distrustful of language" ("a gun means what it says"). Heydrich then takes Kritzinger aside and, advising him to be practical, warns him about his continued opposition. Kritzinger agrees to support him, but gives Heydrich a salutory warning in the form of a story, which Heydrich will relate to Müller and Eichmann once

the meeting has ended. Neumann and Müller again debate labor versus evacuation priorities; Müller says that the priorities have now been set, even by Göring.

The meeting reconvenes. Eichmann reveals the potential of the new stationary gas chambers for industrialized processing and disposal. Meyer calculates the murder rate once the stationary gas chambers and crematoria are in full operation. Heydrich concludes the discussion of what he calls the application of American assembly line methods to this "triumphant German vision." He calls on the attendees, "Link arms, your units, your ministries, apply your intelligence, apply your energies. The machinery is waiting; feed it, get them on the trains, keep the trains rolling, and history will honor us for having the will and the vision to advance the human race to greater purity in a space of time so short Charles Darwin would be astonished." The meeting ends with Heydrich invoking the *Führerprinzip* to resolve any remaining uncertainties about definition, organization, or command. There is a show of unanimous support. The participants leave. Eichmann is left to collect and burn the notes left behind and to take charge of the stenographic rolls from which he and Gunther will begin to construct the Protocol the next day. For the last time, Bühler and Meyer plead for Poland to be given priority (Heydrich refuses). The three RSHA (Reich Security Main Office) leaders (Heydrich, Muller, and Eichmann) retire for drinks. Heydrich tells them Kritzinger's story that warns of the all-consuming nature of hate. As the house staff clean up, each of the participants reappears with his fate printed below the actor's face. As Eichmann drives away, the narrator recounts Eichmann's creation of the Protocol, Heydrich's assassination, and Eichmann's subsequent role in the Holocaust. "Eichmann, as Heydrich's deputy, was left to finish what they had begun at Wannsee. He considered it a matter of honor."

IDEAS FOR CLASS DISCUSSION

The sheer horror of seeing a group of bureaucrats at a meeting calmly discussing the annihilation of huge numbers of people while dining and drinking may seem surrealistic to your students. Yet, sadly enough, it did happen. There is much that can be discussed about the Wannsee Conference and its resulting Protocol. Note with students the complicated racial policies of the Nazis—the degrees of "Jewishness." What policies had already been attempted to make Germany *Judenfrei* by January 1942? With the German conquest of the eastern territories, why did the Jews there appear to present a problem? The Germans had always regarded Slavs and other people to the east as being unclean and sources of disease. This had been articulated during World War I, and even earlier. How was this expressed at the conference? "Who knew what?" is always a thorny question when dealing with the Holocaust. How did this conference deal with the issue of responsibility? How did the language used and the need for secrecy tend to blur what was really being decided? The Protocol text itself can serve as a primary source to help students evaluate the faithfulness of the film's dialogue.

BOOKS AND MATERIALS RELATING TO THIS FILM AND TOPIC

Bankier, David, ed. *Probing the Depths of German Antisemitism: German Society and the Persecution of the Jews, 1933–1941* (Jerusalem: Berghahn Books, Yad Vashem, and the Leo Baeck Institute, 2000).

Bartov, Omer. *Murder in our Midst: The Holocaust, Industrial Killing, and Representation* (Oxford University Press, 1996).

Browning, Christopher. *Nazi Policy, Jewish Workers, German Killers* (Cambridge University Press, 2000).

Burleigh, Michael. *Death and Deliverance: Euthanasia in Germany 1900–1945* (Cambridge University Press, 1994).

_____, ed. *Ethics and Extermination: Reflections on Nazi Genocide* (Cambridge University Press, 1997).

_____ and Wolfgang Wippermann. *The Racial State: Germany 1933–1945* (Cambridge University Press, 1991).

Dwork, Debórah, and Jan van Pelt. *Holocaust: A History* (W. W. Norton, 2002).

Fleming, Gerald. *Hitler and the Final Solution* (University of California Press, 1982).

Johnson, Eric A. *Nazi Terror: The Gestapo, Jews, and Ordinary Germans* (Basic Books, 1999).

Kogon, Eugen; Hermann Langbein; and Adalbert Rückerl, eds. *Nazi Mass Murder: A Documentary History of the Use of Poison Gas* (Yale University Press, 1993).

Lifton, Robert J. *The Nazi Doctors: Medical Killing and the Psychology of Genocide* (Basic Books, 1986).

Marrus, Michael R. *The Holocaust in History* (Penguin-Meridian, 1987).

Rhodes, Richard. *Masters of Death: The SS Einsatzgruppen and the Invention of the Holocaust* (Alfred A. Knopf, 2002).

Roseman, Mark. *The Wannsee Conference and the Final Solution: A Reconsideration* (Metropolitan Books, Henry Holt and Company, 2002).

Weindling, Paul Julius. *Epidemic and Genocide in Eastern Europe: 1890–1945* (Oxford University Press, 2000).

OTHER MEDIA RESOURCES FOR THIS TIME PERIOD

Anne Frank (2001, 189 minutes) This television miniseries was based on Melissa Muller's biography and is notable for its authenticity.

Escape from Sobibor (1987, 120 minutes) This is a dramatization of the largest prisoner escape during World War II, from the Sobibor death camp in Poland.

Holocaust (1978, 463 minutes) This television mini-series follows one Jewish family through Nazi rule in Germany to extermination.

House on Garibaldi Street (1979, 100 minutes) This made-for-television movie depicts the attempts to find Adolf Eichmann and bring him to justice in Israel.

Judgment at Nuremberg (1961, 178 minutes) This is a classic film about the postwar trial of leading Nazis for crimes against humanity.

Miracle at Midnight (1998, 88 minutes) A Disney film, this portrays the transporting of Danish Jews to safety during World War II.

Nuremberg (2000, 180 minutes) This is a Turner Network adaptation of Joseph Persico's novel *Nuremberg: Trial of Infamy*.

The Pianist (2002, 148 minutes) Academy Award-winning film about the survival of Wladyslaw Szpilman, pianist and Polish Jew, in the ruins of Nazi-occupied Warsaw; rated **R**

Playing for Time (1980, 150 minutes) The true story of Fania Fenelon's efforts to form an orchestra in the death camp of Auschwitz as a means of survival is portrayed here.

Schindler's List (1993, 197 minutes) Stephen Spielberg's Academy Award-winning film tells the story of Nazi industrialist Oscar Schindler and his efforts to save his Jewish workers from the death camps. This is a controversial film in many ways; it must be remembered that the story represents only one event in the Holocaust and concerned only a very small number of people. Rated **R**

Varian's War (2000, 120 minutes) This recounts the true story of American journalist Varian Fry (played by William Hurt), who rescued hundreds of prominent cultural figures from Nazi persecution.

CONSPIRACY

HBO Films, 2001; directed by Frank Pierson

Major Character	Actor/Actress
Lt. Colonel Adolf Eichmann [4]	Stanley Tucci
Dr. Joseph Bühler [2]	Ben Daniels
SS Major Rudolf Lange [4]	Barnaby Kay
SS Colonel Eberhard Schöngarth [4]	Peter Sullivan
SS Lt. General Otto Hoffmann [3]	Nicholas Woodeson
Martin Luther [1]	Kevin McNally
Dr. Wilhelm Stuckart [1]	Colin Firth
Dr. Erich Neumann [1]	Jonathan Coy
Dr. Wilhelm Kritzinger [1]	David Threlfall
Dr. Gerhard Klopfer [3]	Ian McNeice
SS General Heinrich Müller [4]	Brendan Coyle
Dr. Roland Freisler [1]	Owen Teale
Dr. Georg Liebbrandt [2]	Ewan Stewart
Dr. Alfred Meyer [2]	Brian Pettifer
SS General Reinhard Heydrich [4]	Kenneth Branagh

Lt. Colonel Adolf Eichmann—Reich Security Main Office, Director Section IVB4, Jewish Affairs. Arrested in Argentina by Israeli Agents, 1962. Tried and executed in Jerusalem, 1962. Eichmann's deputy, Rolf Günther—played in the film by Simon Marker—may have been the meeting note-taker.

Dr. Joseph Bühler—Hans Frank's deputy. Served as State Secretary, General Gouvernement of German Occupied Poland (Cracow). Arrested for war crimes, 1945; released. Died 1982.

SS Major Rudolf Lange—Deputy Commander, SS forces in Latvia (KdS) and *Einsatzkommando* 2 head. Killed in action, Poznan, Poland, 1945.

(continued)

SS Colonel Eberhard Schöngarth—Security Police and Security Service (BdS), General Gouvernement of German Occupied Poland. Convicted by the British of running an unauthorized terror program; executed February 1946.

SS Lt. General Otto Hoffmann—Race and Resettlement Main Office. Arrested 1945; sentenced to 25 years, served six. Died 1982.

Martin Luther—Successful businessman. Joined the Nazi Party in 1932; followed Ribbentrop into the Foreign Ministry, where he served as undersecretary. Sent to Sachenhausen concentration camp for conspiracy against his boss in 1944. Died of a heart attack in 1945. It was his copy of the Protocol that was recovered in 1947 from Foreign Ministry files.

Dr. Wilhelm Stuckart—Wilhelm Frick's deputy, State Secretary Interior Ministry. Was coauthor of the 1935 Nuremberg Laws. Arrested 1945. Convicted, 1949; sentenced to time served. Died in an auto crash in 1953.

Dr. Erich Neumann—Director, Office of the Plenipotentiary Four Year Plan; Göring's representative. Arrested, released, and died 1945.

Dr. Wilhelm Kritzinger—Ministerial Director, Reich Chancellery (headed by Heinrich Lammers), which controlled access to Hitler until supplanted by Martin Bormann in 1943. Was the oldest person at the conference. Arrested in 1945, tried at Nuremberg, declared himself ashamed of Nazi atrocities. Died 1947.

Dr. Gerhard Klopfer —Permanent Secretary, Nazi Party Chancellery; Martin Bormann's deputy. Arrested 1945; released. Died 1987.

SS General Heinrich Müller—Weimar civil servant who came to Himmler's attention as an effective bureaucrat. Joined the Nazi Party in 1938; became Heydrich's deputy and head of the Reich Security Main Office Amt (department) IV (Gestapo). Last seen in Hitler's bunker on April 2, 1945.

Dr. Roland Freisler—SS and Deputy Director, Ministry of Justice. Later served as president of the notorious People's Court that tried the July 1944 plotters against Hitler. Killed in a Berlin air raid, February 1945.

Dr. Georg Liebbrandt—Political Office, Ministry of Occupied Eastern Territories, representing Alfred Rosenberg. Arrested 1945; released. Worked for an American cultural institute; died 1982.

Dr. Alfred Meyer—Rosenberg's deputy, State Secretary, ministry of eastern Poland, the Baltic, and occupied Russia. Committed suicide, spring 1945.

SS General Reinhard Heydrich—SS Chief of Reichs Security Main Office (RSHA), head of the Security Police and Security Service (SD), and Deputy Reichsprotector, Bohemia and Moravia. Assassinated by British-trained Czech agents, 1943. Suspected of having "Jewish blood"; Heydrich sued for slander anyone who accused him of it.

(continued)

WHAT TO WATCH FOR

One of the most horrifying events of the twentieth century was the Holocaust, the systematic killing of millions of Jews and others whom the Nazis felt were inferior and/or expendable. The Wannsee Conference was held at a home in a Berlin suburb on January 20, 1942. This was where, some historians believe, the final solution to the so-called "Jewish Question" was worked out. The conference was called by SS General Reinhard Heydrich and presided over by Lieutenant Colonel Adolf Eichmann, who was the director of Jewish Affairs in the Reich Security Main Office. (He is shown with the number 4 in the Major Character list above.) Other people at the meeting were German government representatives: SS and Nazi Party officials (3), conquered eastern zone administrators (2), security officials, and members of various government ministries (1). The conference was called at this particular time because the Russian campaign had bogged down. The manpower and food that the Germans hoped for from a quick victory over the Soviets had not occurred. With millions of people to feed in the occupied zones, Heydrich invited these men to the conference to make "all necessary preparations in regard to organizational and technical matters for bringing about a complete solution of the Jewish question in the German sphere of influence in Europe." Some historians believe that this conference was where the decision to annihilate the Jews was made, since other methods of ridding German-occupied territories of Jews had not worked. Other historians believe that the Nazis had *always* planned to murder the Jewish population of occupied Europe, and that this conference only represented the final operational details of that policy. Both historical viewpoints can be interpreted in this film. The true significance of the Wannsee Conference is very controversial.

Note the Nazi use of language in dealing with the "Jewish Question." Many euphemisms are used. For example, the word *evacuation* is used instead of *murder*. There is much talk about euthanasia and sterilization as solutions to rid the population of unwanted elements. Also, the complex racial policies of the Nazis are discussed, such as the degrees of "Jewishness" and who is of mixed blood.

Dr. Stuckart and Dr. Kritzinger are opposed to what is happening at the conference. Stuckart, a coauthor of the Nuremberg Laws, thinks the conference policies violate the law. Kritzinger seems to have more ethical and moral objections. How does Heydrich convince them to withdraw their objections?

(continued)

Heydrich is shown to have been careful to make the wording of what was decided at the conference very obscure. He is very much the master of events, orchestrating the conference and bending its members to his will. Given this, how does Heydrich make it clear that the SS will have a major role to play in carrying out the solution decided at this conference?

Screening Notes

─── CONSPIRACY ───

VOCABULARY

"deportation"

Einsatzgruppen

"emigration"

euthanasia

"evacuation"

Final Solution

Führerprinzip

genocide

greater Germany

Holocaust

Judenfrei

Mischlinge

Schutzstaffeln (Defense/Protection Units)

Sicherheitsdienst (Security Service)

QUESTIONS BASED ON THE FILM AND ON THE PROTOCOL TEXT ON PAGE 150

1. What reasons does Heydrich give for convening the meeting? What other motives do the other participants suggest he has?

   _____

   _____

   _____

   _____

2. What are the burning issues that each of the four groups represented at the meeting (government ministries, conquered zone administrators, SS and party functionaries, Heydrich's RSHA personnel) hope to address?

   _____

   _____

   _____

   _____

(continued)

3. On what do the meeting participants agree? About what do they disagree? In particular, how do Stuckart and Kritzinger formulate their respective disagreements?

_____

_____

_____

_____

4. Based on the film, what kind of person is Heydrich? What kinds of inducements or threats does he employ to achieve his objectives?

_____

_____

_____

5. At the end of the film, the narrator says, "Eichmann, as Heydrich's deputy for Jewish Affairs, was left to finish what they had begun at Wannsee. He considered it a matter of honor." Based on what you see him doing in the film, what are Eichmann's characteristics?

_____

_____

_____

6. Based on your viewing of the film and your reading of the Protocol, how biologically coherent was the German racial ideal?

_____

_____

_____

_____

(continued)

7. What kinds of solutions are proposed for the "Jewish Question"? How are these solutions dealt with in the meeting and the resulting Protocol?

_____

_____

_____

_____

_____

8. How do issues of public reactions, both inside greater Germany and in other countries, get resolved at the meeting?

_____

_____

_____

_____

9. Based on your viewing of the film and your reading of the Protocol, what future did the Jewish people (and others deemed inferior by the Nazis) in greater Germany and occupied Europe have to look forward to?

_____

_____

_____

_____

(continued)

10. The film's narrator begins stating that "[i]n two hours, these men [the Wannsee participants] changed the world forever." Do you agree? Why?

_____

_____

_____

_____

_____

11. In your opinion, does the film believably re-create the conference summarized in the Protocol? Cite specific examples from the Protocol text that support, contradict, or provide no evidence for the setting, actions, or dialogue created by the screenwriter.

_____

_____

_____

_____

_____

World War II

TEACHER'S GUIDE

A BRIDGE TOO FAR

United Artists, 1977; directed by Richard Attenborough, color, 175 minutes

BACKGROUND OF THE FILM

Based on Cornelius Ryan's 1974 best-selling book, *A Bridge Too Far* tells the story of Operation Market-Garden. This was Field Marshal Montgomery's plan to bring World War II to a rapid close by taking the bridges over the Rhine River and moving the Allies into the Ruhr in September 1944. Due to poor intelligence reports, logistics snafus, and just plain bad luck, the operation was a failure. It did not shorten the war; in fact, it provided the Germans with a last victory and added greatly to the casualty figures, with a loss of 17,000 Allied soldiers and perhaps as many as 10,000 Dutch civilians. The title is taken from a quotation by Lieutenant General Frederick Browning, who warned Montgomery, "I think we might be going a bridge too far." That bridge was the one spanning the Rhine at Arnhem, Holland, the ultimate objective of the operation.

Operation Market-Garden involved two phases. The Market phase was an airborne drop behind the German lines. The British 1st Airborne under Major General Urquhart, aided by the Polish Parachute Brigade under General Sosabowski, was to land in the Arnhem area. The U.S. 82nd Airborne under Brigadier General Gavin was to secure the bridges at Grave and Nijmegen. The U.S. 101st Airborne under Major General Maxwell Taylor was to secure the southern area of the ground route near Einhoven. The Garden phase was to be the rapid movement of British ground

forces across the Belgian border into Holland and up the road to Arnhem.

Producer Joseph E. Levine contracted with author Ryan for movie rights four years before the book was finished. Levine budgeted $25 million of his own money on the film, hired British director Richard Attenborough, and stipulated that he wanted big-name stars for the major roles. The shooting for the film began on April 26, 1976, and ended on October 6, 1976. It came in ahead of schedule and, amazingly, under budget.

Many of the key figures in Operation Market-Garden were invited to act as technical advisors. Major General Urquhart, General Gavin, Brigadier Vandeleur, and General Frost were on hand to meet the actors portraying them and to provide information and criticism. The site selected for the on-location shooting was the eighth-century Dutch city of Deventer, only a few miles from Arnhem. Arnhem could not be used, since so much of the city had been destroyed during the war. Over 6,000 uniforms for the American, British, German, Polish, and Dutch troops had to be collected. When only a few operating armored vehicles were found, fiberglass replicas were built. The Horsa gliders that carried in the airborne troops had to be researched and reconstructed; not one remained in existence, nor even a set of plans. Over 500,000 feet of film were shot, to be edited down to a 17,000-foot final version.

The remarkable logistics involved in re-creating the war scenes make this film noteworthy. It does portray the terrible, destructive nature of World War II for both the military and civilian populations. It is interesting to note that this film was one of many

---

about World War II that were produced in the 1970s. Speculation is that in an era reeling from Vietnam, World War II represented a "good" war—one in which the issues were clear-cut, there was a clear distinction between good guys and bad guys, and the United States was on the winning side.* *A Bridge Too Far* represents a kind of heroism and courage that people could easily identify and comprehend in a time when those virtues seemed lost.

*See, for example, Vincent Canby, in *The New York Times,* July 3, 1977.

SYNOPSIS OF THE PLOT

The film opens with black-and-white actuality footage of the D day invasion and a narration that explains Montgomery's plan, Operation Market-Garden. The dramatic action begins in Arnhem, Holland, in September 1944, at the home of a member of the Dutch underground. The family hears the sounds of the German army retreating. At the German western front headquarters, a new commanding officer, Von Rundstedt, has taken charge, and the retreat is stopped. General Bittrich's SS Panzer divisions are moved to Arnhem for a rest stop. At General Browning's headquarters in England, the Allied officers learn about the plans for Operation Market-Garden. The Dutch underground reports German activity in Arnhem, but the British command discounts these reports. As the day gets closer to the parachute drop, problems crop up with finding a drop zone and enough aircraft. General Sosabowski expresses misgivings about the plan. Lieutenant General Horrocks explains the ground operations to the armored division officers.

The day of the drop brings good weather, and the planes are soon over Holland. At the (30th) Corps headquarters, General Horrocks emphasizes that the ground forces must not fall behind schedule. Meanwhile, at General Bittrich's headquarters in Arnhem, the general views the massive air drop. General Ludwig is told he must hold the bridge at Nijmegen. Unfortunately for the Allies, many of their jeeps are

damaged when the gliders land, so the paratroopers must walk to Arnhem.

Meanwhile, the ground forces encounter heavy German resistance. The Allies are victorious, but at a loss of time and equipment. General Urquhart's Red Devils in Arnhem are faced with disastrous equipment problems—none of their radios work. As General Frost's men march toward Arnhem, they are greeted as liberators by the Dutch. The U.S. Airborne arrives at the Son Bridge, but as the men run toward it, the bridge blows up.

The ground forces are six miles from Einhoven. Back at Arnhem, Urquhart meets heavy resistance from the Germans. Frost and his men arrive in Arnhem and take over a private home within view of the bridge. Major Carlyle steps out on the bridge, but he and his men are driven back by sniper fire. At night they try again to take the bridge, accidentally setting the bridge girders on fire. The Germans attempt to cross into Arnhem but are stopped by Frost's forces. The bridge is blocked with burning German tanks. Although Frost holds one end of the bridge, the Germans have him surrounded.

Urquhart and two comrades go to Arnhem to try to reestablish communication with the rest of the paratroopers. They find the city overrun with Germans and find refuge in a Dutch house. Meanwhile, the Polish paratroopers' backup drop has been delayed by poor weather. At Einhoven, things are going better; the entire city is celebrating the arrival of the ground forces under Lieutenant Colonel Vandeleur.

The Americans at Son reconstruct the bridge so the armored divisions can cross, still 39 miles from Arnhem. At Arnhem, the German Panzer divisions retaliate and move into the city. The British airborne takes over the Hartenstein Hotel outside Arnhem, and Urquhart is reunited with his forces. He learns that supplies are short and they are surrounded by the Germans. The pilots are dropping supplies into zones controlled by the Germans. The Allies secure the home of Kate Ter Horst for the wounded. The Germans ask General Frost to surrender. When he refuses, General Bittrich gives the order to flatten Arnhem.

At Nijmegen, the U.S. paratroopers decide to take the bridge by launching an amphibious assault across the Waal River to take both ends of the bridge at once. There are many casualties, but the Americans make it across and secure the other end of the bridge. The Germans try to blow up the bridge, but the explosives do not detonate. The British tanks cross the bridge and head toward Arnhem. At Arnhem, the fighting has become house-to-house. Finally, the Germans succeed; they capture Frost and his exhausted men.

Meanwhile, General Sosabowski and his Polish paratroopers are finally dropped five miles from Arnhem, but with very heavy casualties. They attempt to cross the Rhine to join Urquhart but are driven back. A Dutch physician, Dr. Spaander, asks the Germans for a cease-fire to move the wounded to a safe area. It is granted by General Bittrich.

From a mile away, the Allied officers watch helplessly as the Germans bombard Urquhart's men. Urquhart is given orders to evacuate his able-bodied men. The wounded, doctors, and chaplains are left behind to fire guns and man the radios to keep the Germans from learning of the withdrawal. When the Germans achieve their victory (their last of the war), they find only the British wounded sitting passively and quietly singing.

IDEAS FOR CLASS DISCUSSION

The Allied cooperation pictured in this film would be a good topic for class discussion. One lesson learned from World War I was to establish a coordinated Allied command. The method of warfare used during World War II could also be discussed in relation to World War I as well as to more modern warfare, such as that seen in the Persian Gulf and Afghanistan by U.S. military forces. What changes in weaponry and technology have occurred?

BOOKS AND MATERIALS RELATING TO THIS FILM AND TOPIC

Bauer, Cornelius. *The Battle of Arnhem, Zebra World at War Series, No.17* (Zebra Press, 1979).

A Bridge Too Far, *Movie Spectacular, Vol. 1, No. 1* (Magazine Division of the *New York Times*, 1977).

Leckie, Robert. *Delivered from Evil, The Saga of World War II* (Harper & Row, 1987).

MacDonald, Charles B. *The Mighty Endeavor, American Armed Forces in the European Theatre in World War II* (Oxford University Press, 1969).

Ryan, Cornelius. *A Bridge Too Far* (Popular Library, 1977).

OTHER MEDIA RESOURCES FOR THIS TIME PERIOD

Empire of the Sun (1987, 154 minutes) This Steven Spielberg film portrays a young, privileged English boy who tries to survive the Japanese invasion of Shanghai and confinement to a POW camp.

Enemy at the Gates (2001, 131 minutes) A film about the Siege of Stalingrad, it covers an important turning point in the war. Rated **R**

The Longest Day (1962, 180 minutes) This big-budget picture re creates the Allied invasion of Normandy.

Midway (1976, 132 minutes) This film has an all-star cast and accurately portrays the naval battle that shifted the balance of power in the Pacific.

Paradise Road (1997, 122 minutes) Women from different countries and backgrounds are interned in a Japanese POW camp in Indonesia. One of them begins a vocal orchestra to pass the time and relieve the pain of their brutal conditions. Rated **R**

Patton (1970, 169 minutes) This is an Academy Award-winning picture about one of World War II's most controversial generals.

Saving Private Ryan (1998, 175 minutes) This is an Academy Award-winning movie about three brothers who are killed during World War II. The U.S. government sets out to find the fourth brother, who is somewhere behind enemy lines. Rated **R**

Tora! Tora! Tora! (1970, 143 minutes) An American-Japanese collaboration, this film recounts the events leading up to and including Pearl Harbor. It is a very technically accurate re-creation.

A Town Like Alice (1956, 135 minutes) Women and children in Malaya are captured by the Japanese army and have to walk for months from POW camp to POW camp. The main character meets an Australian POW from Alice Springs, who befriends her. After the war, she tries to find him and begin a new life in the Australian outback.

World War II

A BRIDGE TOO FAR

United Artists, 1977; directed by Richard Attenborough

Major Character	Actor/Actress
Lt. Gen. Frederick Browning	Dirk Bogarde
Maj. Gen. Robert Urquhart	Sean Connery
Lt. Gen. Brian Horrocks	Edward Fox
Brig. Gen. James Gavin	Ryan O'Neal
Maj. Gen. Stanislaw Sosabowski	Gene Hackman
Lt. Col. JOE. Vandeleur	Michael Caine
Lt. Gen. John Frost	Anthony Hopkins
Col. Bobby Stout	Elliott Gould
Staff Sgt. Charles Dohun	James Caan
Kate Ter Horst	Liv Ullmann
Maj. Julian Cook	Robert Redford
Dr. Spaander	Laurence Olivier

WHAT TO WATCH FOR

Based on Cornelius Ryan's 1974 best-selling book, *A Bridge Too Far* tells the story of Operation Market-Garden. This was Field Marshal Montgomery's plan to bring World War II to a rapid close in September 1944. The plan was to take the bridges over the Rhine River and move the Allied forces into the Ruhr, an industrial area of Germany. Due to poor intelligence reports, logistics snafus, and just plain bad luck, the operation was a failure. It did not shorten the war. Instead, it added greatly to the casualty figures, with a loss of 17,000 Allied soldiers and perhaps as many as 10,000 Dutch civilians. Operation Market-Garden involved two phases. The Market phase was an airborne drop behind the German lines. The Garden phase was to be a rapid movement of British ground forces across the Belgian border into Holland.

(continued)

From there, they were to move up to the final bridge across the Rhine at Arnhem.

Watch for the cooperation among the Allied forces. Also note the objectives of the operation and the major coordination and logistics the operation required. Imagine even the complications of producing this movie. Visualize the numbers of extras necessary in scenes such as the parachute drop. Think about the expense involved in the collection and/or reconstruction of World War II vintage equipment and over 6,000 uniforms. (The film was budgeted at $25 million.)

Note the destructive nature of World War II for both the military and civilian populations. The city of Arnhem was so badly destroyed during the war that it could not be used as a location site for the film. The city of Deventer, Holland, only a few miles from Arnhem, was used instead. Many of the key figures who participated in Operation Market-Garden acted as technical advisors for the film. Major General Urquhart, General Gavin, Brigadier Vandeleur, and General Frost were able to meet the actors portraying them and provide information and criticism.

Screening Notes

A BRIDGE TOO FAR

VOCABULARY

Allied forces   paratroopers
civilians   RAF
Luftwaffe   SS
Operation Market-Garden   the underground

QUESTIONS BASED ON THE FILM

1. What is the ultimate objective of Operation Market-Garden?

   _____

   _____

   _____

2. Why is Major Fuller sent on sick leave?

   _____

   _____

   _____

3. Why are gliders used in the air drop?

   _____

   _____

   _____

(continued)

4. Comment on the cooperation among the Allied forces as shown in the film.

_____

_____

_____

_____

_____

5. How do the Dutch civilians fight back against the Germans?

_____

_____

_____

_____

6. How does Urquhart fool the Germans during his evacuation of the paratroopers?

_____

_____

_____

_____

World War II: The Home Front

TEACHER'S GUIDE

HOPE AND GLORY

Columbia Pictures Corporation, 1987; directed by John Boorman, color, 118 minutes. Nominated for an Academy Award for Best Picture.

BACKGROUND OF THE FILM

A major war affects not only the combatants, but also those left behind on the home front. Nowhere was this more evident than in Britain during World War II. After the surrender of France to Nazi Germany on June 22, 1940, Britain fought on—and, for a while, it fought on alone. Soon after the war began, Winston Churchill became the prime minister of a coalition government that dedicated itself to rallying the entire population to support the war effort. Churchill stated that he could promise the British people nothing but "blood, toil, tears, and sweat" in their ordeal. The British people responded in an unprecedented manner. There were no protests against conscription, as had occurred during the first World War; men of all ages rushed to join the armed forces. Women took their places in industry and agriculture, and those men too old to fight joined the Home Guard or became Air Raid Patrol Wardens. Even Princess Elizabeth (later Queen Elizabeth II) drove an ambulance.

This film spans the first three years of World War II in Britain as seen through the eyes of a nine-year-old boy, Billy. The film begins with Prime Minister Neville Chamberlain announcing the beginning of war with Germany; it ends with Winston Churchill's speech on the Allied victory at El Alamein. The family of the main character is pictured as typical, with three

children and a terrace house outside London. The film is based on the reminiscences of the director, John Boorman; Billy is probably meant to be Boorman himself. Here, Boorman is not really concerned with the overall tragedy of war, but only with how the war is experienced by one little boy. When the air-raid siren sounds at school, the children are less concerned about their immediate safety than about getting out of their daily lessons to go to an air-raid shelter. This may well have been the reality of wartime for most children. Their ability to find excitement in pieces of shrapnel, barrage balloons, and bombed-out houses shows us something about the resilience of youth.

Hope and Glory is an accurate re-creation of the sights and sounds of this time period, particularly of the restrictions and shortages faced by the population. The main characters are shown wearing the same clothes in different scenes, reflecting wartime shortages. In one scene, the family goes to a clothing exchange, where they can swap their own used clothing for different used clothing. Dawn has Billy draw lines on her legs so that people will think she is wearing seamed stockings. When Clive enlists, he puts the family car up on blocks to be stored for the duration of the war due to the strict petrol rationing. When a German pilot is forced to parachute into the neighborhood after his plane is shot down, what the women scramble to recover is the parachute silk, highly prized for clothing. The pilot is taken prisoner of war by an elderly MP, who tells him to mind the brussels sprouts as they walk through a Victory garden. (Food shortages were very serious during the war. Every family depended on ration coupons for essentials like tea, sugar, butter, meat, and bread. Victory gardens could supplement the meager diet with fresh vegetables; brussels sprouts grew well and nearly all year long. Americans stationed in Britain during the war swore that once the war was over, they would never eat brussels sprouts again.)

The family builds what has been termed an Anderson shelter in their backyard. These were commonly constructed for use during air raids in areas where people could not make it to underground (subway) tunnels, which were used in the city of London during air raids. Gas masks were distributed to children at school out of fear that the Germans would use poisonous gas, as they had during World War I. The barrage balloon, a source of fun for the children in the film, was anchored in many neighborhoods to snag low-flying German planes on their wires. Patriotism and affection for the royal family are shown accurately in the film, as is the king's stutter, which made him seem more endearing and human to many of his subjects.

The war was a great social leveler in Britain, as people from all walks of life experienced the same hardships. There was some black market trading and corruption, but most people accepted the restrictions with a sense of egalitarianism. As people, particularly children, were evacuated from the cities to rural areas, people from different regions of the nation got to know each other. Full employment returned after the poor conditions of the 1920s and 1930s. Importantly, there was a sense that once the war was won, the British government would need to take responsibility for the well-being of its citizens. Wartime sacrifices should be rewarded, not simply replaced by conditions of economic depression and social dislocation.

In the middle of the war, the Beveridge Report of 1942 outlined plans for a comprehensive system of social security; it included universal health insurance, unemployment insurance, and old-age pensions. This eventually set up a social welfare system that took care of people from "cradle to grave." In the film, note the discussion between Clive and Mac when they are visiting the bomb site with Billy. They express their discontentment with the way the system has treated them in the past, particularly as veterans of the 1914 war. This feeling was quite widespread in Great Britain and was instrumental in pressuring the government to be more proactive after this war than it had been in 1918.

A few things in the movie might confuse American audiences. For example, Clive and his friends are often heard to say, "Steady the Buffs!" This is the motto of the Royal East Kent Regiment, in which these characters served during World War I. The "googly" is a cricket pitch. According to the established Church of England at that time, public schools had daily prayers and hymns. Also, on most world maps of that era, the British Empire appeared either in red or pink. An important part of every English Christmas dinner is, even to this day, the king's or queen's Christmas message broadcast. Finally, moviemaking was encouraged during World War II to keep up public morale, although there was government censorship.

SYNOPSIS OF THE PLOT

Billy lives in a typical middle-class London neighborhood of terrace houses. On a beautiful September day in 1939, war is declared against Germany, and Billy's world is about to change drastically. The family includes Mum and Dad (Grace and Clive), older sister Dawn, and younger sister Sue; they all begin to prepare for the war. A bomb shelter is constructed in the back garden, and the car is put up on blocks for the duration. Grace considers sending her younger children to relatives in Australia to get them out of the war zone, but at the last minute she cannot bring herself to do so. Clive has enlisted in the army, despite Grace's trepidations.

The scene switches to a later time, when the Battle of Britain is in full force. Billy's house is fitted with blackout curtains; air raids are a nightly occurrence. The children go to school carrying their gas masks, and the headmaster exhorts them to pray for "victory to the righteous." A barrage balloon is moored over Billy's neighborhood to entrap enemy planes in the cables. When several houses on the street are hit by bombs, the neighborhood boys turn them into play areas where they can collect shrapnel and shells. They also contribute to the destruction by smashing what little is left of the houses.

When a dogfight occurs in the skies over the neighborhood, a German pilot is shot down and parachutes into a yard. Everyone comes out to stare. An elderly policeman arrests the pilot, who seems almost relieved to be taken away. The women cut up the parachute silk for clothing. Meanwhile, Dawn is caught up in a relationship with Bruce, a young Canadian soldier stationed nearby.

When Clive comes home on leave, he brings a jar of German jam, which has washed up ashore from a sunken ship. The family is reluctant to eat it, but eventually they do. The balloon escapes from its mooring and is shot by members of the Home Guard (sometimes humorously referred to as Dad's Army). Deprivations on the home front are shown by the clothing exchange, where women go to get "new" old clothing to wear. Christmas finds the family together listening to the king's Christmas message, often a trying experience due to George VI's stutter.

As a break from the war, Grace and the younger children go to the beach with Clive's friend Mac. When they return, they find that their house has burned. After discovering that Dawn is safe, Grace is most concerned that her ration books have been left in the ruined house. When the gang of boys plays "total destruction" in Billy's burned-out home, he chases them away in anger. The family moves in with Grace's mother and rather eccentric father on the banks of the Thames, seemingly far removed from the destruction of London.

Dawn tells her mother that she is expecting a baby. Bruce goes AWOL to be with Dawn, and they are married. After the wedding, Bruce is taken off by the Military Police. Dawn has her baby. Billy spends a carefree summer on the river, but he has to return to his old school for the next term. His grandfather

grudgingly drives him there using his last bit of "black market petrol," but when the children enter the schoolyard, they find that the school building has been totally destroyed by a bomb. The film ends with a voice-over saying that this extra period of freedom is the best thing that happens to Billy during the war.

IDEAS FOR CLASS DISCUSSION

This film lends itself to a discussion of government involvement in the lives of its citizens. After the war, the British public expected a more proactive approach to their social and economic problems. The 1942 Beveridge Report outlined plans for a welfare state, including national health insurance, which would provide "cradle to grave" security for citizens once the war was won. Why did the war create demands for this sort of approach? A discussion of the kind of deprivations that civilians can face during a war might be fruitful. After the terrorist attacks of September 11, 2001, in the United States, the increased security restrictions frustrated some Americans. Would citizens today be as resilient in facing rationing and restrictions on their freedom of movement as they were during World War II?

BOOKS AND MATERIALS RELATING TO THIS FILM AND TOPIC

Barber, John, and Mark Harrison. *The Soviet Home Front, 1941–1945: A Social and Economic History of the USSR in World War II* (Addison-Wesley Publishing Company, 1991).

Beck, Earl R. *Under the Bombs: The German Home Front, 1942–1945* (University Press of Kentucky, 1999).

Briggs, Asa. *Go To It: Victory on the Home Front, 1939–1945* (Mitchell Beazley, 2000).

Gregory, Jenny, ed. *On the Home Front: Western Australia and World War II* (University of Western Australia Press, 2000).

OTHER MEDIA RESOURCES FOR THIS TIME PERIOD

Au Revoir les Enfants (1987, 104 minutes) Based on director Louis Malle's personal experiences, this film focuses on a Catholic-run boarding school in France during World War II and how the boys there deal with surrounding events.

Bridge to the Sun (1961, 113 minutes) This film is based on the autobiography of an American woman who married a Japanese diplomat and spent the war living in Japan.

Dark Blue World (2001, 114 minutes) Czech pilots flee their homeland during World War II and join the RAF. This film cuts between wartime Britain and postwar Czechoslovakia under Soviet rule. Rated **R**

Land Girls (1998, 110 minutes) In 1941, three young women from different backgrounds join a new British regiment, the Land Army, moving to the countryside to work on farms. Rated **R**

Mrs. Miniver (1942, 134 minutes) This film won seven Academy Awards. It was considered a powerful piece of propaganda and a morale booster for the British war effort. A middle-class wife attempts to hold her family together during the early years of World War II and demonstrates British resilience during a time of hardship and crisis.

The Night of the Shooting Stars (1982, 105 minutes) A recollection from the director's childhood, this film is shown in flashback through the eyes of a six-year-old girl. Italian villagers try to thwart the Nazis and find the American troops sent to liberate them. Rated **R**

World War II: The Home Front

HOPE AND GLORY

Columbia Pictures Corporation, 1987; directed by John Boorman

Major Character	Actor/Actress
Billy	Sebastian Rice-Edwards
Sue	Geraldine Muir
Dawn	Sammi Davis
Grace	Sarah Miles
Clive	David Hayman
Mac	Derrick O'Connor
Molly	Susan Wooldridge
Bruce	Jean-Marc Barr
Grandfather	Ian Bannen

WHAT TO WATCH FOR

This film is a reminiscence of director John Boorman's childhood in London during World War II. Thus, the war is seen through the eyes of a nine-year-old boy living with his family in a typical middle-class suburban neighborhood. The filmmakers have tried to carefully re-create wartime Britain. The time span of the movie is from the declaration of war by Prime Minister Neville Chamberlain in September 1939 to the Allied victory at El Alamein in October 1942. It is important to remember that until the United States entered the war in December 1941, Britain fought Germany alone. The British public had to make unprecedented sacrifices to wage "total war" against Germany. Everyone's efforts were turned toward winning the war; the rationing of food, clothing, and fuel was widespread. Also, although the British started regular television service in 1936, it was discontinued at the outbreak of war. The radio was, therefore, the most important form of communication.

(continued)

Although people really knew better, they expressed an optimistic and patriotic feeling that the war would be over soon, "before Christmas . . . ."

Note the scene that depicts the beginning of the war. There is almost a sense of disbelief that it is really happening. (Only a little over 20 years have passed since the end of World War I.) London and other urban industrial areas, like Coventry, took the brunt of the bombing during the Battle of Britain. This was known as the "blitz" from *blitzkrieg,* the German word for "lightning war." Although the British were subject to bombing throughout the war, first by the Luftwaffe and later by V-1 buzz bombs and V-2 missiles, the Battle of Britain was the most dramatic. It took place between August 13 and September 30, 1940, as a "softening-up" operation for the Germans. They were preparing the way for an invasion across the English Channel known as Operation Sea Lion. The German failure during the Battle of Britain, and British bombing operations against the German-controlled French harbors where the enemy was preparing for the invasion, caused Hitler to call off Sea Lion on September 17.

Every area in Britain had an air-raid shelter. In their back gardens, families constructed Anderson shelters like the one built by Billy's father. Children were issued gas masks at school because the British were afraid that the Germans would use poison gas, as they did during World War I. Note that the only men left around are elderly. They made up the ranks of the Air Raid Wardens and the Home Guard.

In the film, the German parachutist is told to "mind the brussels sprouts." People in Britain grew as much of their own food as they could. Since brussels sprouts grow practically all year long, they were a staple in many people's wartime diets. (Americans who were stationed in Britain swore they would never ever eat brussels sprouts again.) Consumer goods were also very scarce—no jam, butter, clothes, or stockings. Ration books were precious and guarded carefully. Dawn has Billy paint seams on her legs to make it appear as if she is wearing stockings. Clothing exchanges were held where people traded their old clothes for different old clothes. Note the sense of community and sharing shown by the citizens, who are all suffering the same hardships.

There was a strong sense of patriotism and affection for the royal family. In the film, the family stands for the playing of "God Save the King" on the radio at Christmas dinner. George VI was a popular king, despite his shyness and bad stutter.

(continued)

His wife, Queen Elizabeth, was thought by Hitler to be the most dangerous woman in Europe, because she worked so hard keeping up British morale during the blitz.

Petrol (gasoline) was severely rationed. Clive puts the family car on blocks for the duration of the war, and Grandfather complains about driving Billy into London to go to school. Note the film crew in this final scene. Movies continued to be produced and shot during World War II in most industrialized countries. It was felt that movies helped the war effort by providing entertainment and boosting morale. The studios generally worked with their governments, and movies were often subject to censorship.

Screening Notes

World War II: The Home Front

HOPE AND GLORY

VOCABULARY

Air Raid Patrol Warden

Anderson shelter

barrage balloon

blitz

gas masks

Home Guard

rationing

shrapnel

QUESTIONS BASED ON THE FILM

1. How does life change for Billy as the war progresses?

_____

_____

_____

_____

_____

2. What deprivations are faced by the Rohan family during the war?

_____

_____

_____

_____

_____

(continued)

3. What steps does the British Government take to protect the civilian population and wage "total war"?

_____

_____

_____

_____

4. How does the character of Grace change as the film progresses? How does this represent the change in the role of women that occurred during the war?

_____

_____

_____

_____

_____

5. What differences are there between Billy's school and your school and classroom today?

_____

_____

_____

_____

6. Some critics have felt that this movie sentimentalizes World War II too much. They think that the plot is based only on the director's selective memory. Do you agree? Why or why not?

_____

_____

_____

_____

_____

(continued)

7. The theme song heard throughout the movie and during the closing credits is "Land of Hope and Glory." This is better known to Americans as "Pomp and Circumstance," which is often played at graduations. The words of "Land of Hope and Glory" are:

> Land of Hope and Glory
> Mother of the Free
> How shall we extol thee
> Who are born of thee?
> Wider still and wider
> Shall thy bounds be set
> God, who made thee mighty
> Make thee mightier yet . . .
> God, who made thee mighty
> Make thee mightier yet.

Why might this song be meaningful for British citizens during World War II?

_____

_____

_____

_____

_____

_____

TEACHER'S GUIDE

XIU XIU: THE SENT DOWN GIRL

(sometimes listed as *Tian yu*)
Stratosphere Entertainment Presentation of
a Whispering Steppes LP Production, 1998;
directed by Joan Chen, color, 99 minutes. In
Chinese with English subtitles; rated **R** for
sexual content.

BACKGROUND OF THE FILM

The history of China in the twentieth century has
been chaotic, as the world's most populous nation has
attempted to find a stable economic, social, and political structure as well as establish its place in the world
order. One of the most devastating events to take
place during this era was Mao Zedong's Cultural
Revolution, which began in 1966.

As Mao aged, he became concerned that China
would engage in what he considered "Soviet revision-
ism" and would not adhere to his policies. To ensure
revolutionary fervor and continue his legacy, he insti-
tuted the Cultural Revolution. Party members, many
of whom were high-ranking, were purged; government officials who were thought to lack revolutionary
zeal were removed. Mao turned to the youth of
China, mobilizing millions of students and young
people to join the Red Guard to carry his message
to the nation. Unleashed and given great freedom by
their leader, the Red Guard converged on the cities
and villages of China. They terrorized and demeaned
government, party, and educational officials and
attempted to destroy all remnants of bourgeois life.

Mao believed that the peasant was the true proletariat. To "educate" city dwellers about the honest

simplicity of rural life, he sent educators, profession-
als, party members, and other city dwellers to
perform forced labor in the country. This was a disaster; the educational system of China broke down, and
the economy suffered. Millions of people were sent
to labor camps, and thousands lost their lives in the
turmoil and poor conditions.

Between 1967 and 1976, approximately 7.5 million
Chinese youth were "sent down" for training to
remote areas in the Chinese countryside. Some never
returned to their homes and were never heard from
again. The peasants resented the urban workers and
treated them with hostility and contempt. Instead of
lessening the gap between rural and urban people, the
Cultural Revolution only exacerbated their differences. Nevertheless, although later leadership criti-
cized Mao's blunders, he remains to this day an iconic
figure who led China from being a victim of imperialism to emerging as a world power.

It is against this background that the story of *Xiu
Xiu: The Sent Down Girl* is told. Wenxiu (Xiu Xiu is her
nickname) is a 15-year-old who lives in the provincial
city of Chengdu. Even though the year is 1975,
remnants of the Cultural Revolution are still evident;
Mao is still alive. It is still considered appropriate to
"reeducate" urban citizens by sending them to live
with the rural proletariat members and do "honest"
work in the countryside.

This film was shot on location in China without
the approval of the Chinese government. It is based
on a novella, *Heavenly Bath,* written by Geling Yan.
This is the debut film of director Joan Chen. Chen
was born in China and, ironically, was discovered by

World History on the Screen

Mao's wife, who sent her to a film producer. Chen was a much-applauded actress in China before moving to the United States in the early 1980s, where she became known as the Chinese Elizabeth Taylor. Chen filmed in remote locations, thus concealing her work; the movie was made without interference from government officials. The film has been banned in China, however, and Chen has been barred from making any more films there.

This film includes some scenes of sexual encounters that are fairly important to the plot. They are not as explicit as in many films seen by teenagers today, but they can be skipped fairly easily with adequate explanation. Make clear to students that Xiu Xiu, in her innocence, is being exploited. Her situation demonstrates the corruption inherent in the Cultural Revolution and the breakdown of morals in the Chinese government during this time.

SYNOPSIS OF THE PLOT

The film opens with graphics explaining the Cultural Revolution and indicating that 7.5 million students were "sent down" to the countryside as part of Mao's grand plan. The opening scene is in Chengdu; the year is 1975. A loudspeaker is blaring as schoolchildren exercise in the schoolyard to the broadcast instructions. A voice-over by a young male student says that this is the day when he and Wenxiu leave their childhood.

The scene switches to Wenxiu's home, where she is taking a bath. Her mother explains that she has gone to great trouble to get extra supplies, like toilet paper, for Wenxiu's journey. Xiu Xiu (her nickname) meets her boyfriend. She excitedly tells him that she has signed up for training, because it is like being in the army; they will even get uniforms. They agree to write. The boy gives her a kaleidoscope as a farewell gift. Xiu Xiu's father is a tailor. He sews blouses for her to take to the countryside.

Xiu Xiu and her friends are lined up and ready to leave on buses and trucks. They are given army coats, and their hands are stamped. Her boyfriend has permission to stay behind through the influence of

friends and family. The families wave goodbye as the girls leave for their "adventure."

One year later, young people are watching a black-and-white movie outdoors at a training camp. Disagreements break out when the young women accuse the young men of touching them. One girl, Xiu Xiu's friend Chen Li, is lost, never to be found. In a voice-over, the boyfriend back at home says that he rarely hears from Xiu Xiu.

At the camp headquarters, Xiu Xiu is told that she is an exemplary worker. She is being sent to learn how to train horses for the White River Iron Girls' Cavalry. Xiu Xiu is introduced to Lao Jin, an expert marksman as well as a skilled horseman. Xiu Xiu is driven out to Lao Jin's camp on the Tibetan steppes. She is told that at an early age, Lao Jin "lost his manhood" during a Tibetan tribal war; thus he cannot marry or have children. She will be safe with him. When she arrives, Xiu Xiu is shocked to learn that Lao Jin only has one tent, and that she will have to share it with him. Xiu Xiu is very nervous about undressing and washing in the presence of Lao Jin. He is careful to look the other way, saying, "All you Chengdu girls like to wash."

While out herding horses, Xiu Xiu explains that she has been useful at the factory but doesn't know anything here. She tells Lao Jin that he probably hasn't bathed a day in his life. She wonders why he has no watch or working radio, as the other herders have. Lao Jin begins to dig a large hole, which he then lines with rocks and tarps—it is a bath for Xiu Xiu. She is thrilled, but worried that someone will see her. When some herders pass by, Lao Jin scares them off.

After six months pass, Xiu Xiu misses her family and life in Chengdu. She has heard that Chen Li has been taken away to be married and now has a child. Xiu Xiu says that she would rather die than spend her life in a place like this. She realizes that she has been here for 180 days and that headquarters has promised to come and get her. She dresses in a nice sweater and scarf and waits for someone to arrive. No one comes. Lao Jin announces that they will need to move camp to find fresh water. Xiu Xiu is sure that no one will ever find her if they move.

While Lao Jin is out herding, Xiu Xiu meets a peddler with a yak cart. He tells her that the girls' cavalry has long been disbanded and that they are all trying to get home. Headquarters is swamped; girls whose parents have money and connections are getting the precious permits to leave and return home. Xiu Xiu tells him that she does not know anyone. The peddler convinces Xiu Xiu that he has influence. Everyone knows him; he has the power and the "goods." He tells Xiu Xiu that she is an honest girl who hasn't "visited" the chiefs at headquarters to earn favors. He tells Xiu Xiu to visit him at the headquarters. The peddler later returns and asks why Xiu Xiu has not come to the movie at headquarters. He promises her that they will go to Chengdu together as he undresses her and they have sex.

Xiu Xiu continues to wait for someone to come and get her. She tries to convince Lao Jin to ride to the Saturday movie at headquarters. When he refuses, she tries to ride there by herself, but her horse runs away. She is rescued by Lao Jin.

A man on a motorbike comes by the tent; he has gotten directions from the peddler. He says that he sends girls back to Chengdu all the time. He also has sex with Xiu Xiu while Lao Jin is out working. When Lao Jin returns, he suspects what has happened. He rides a long distance to get Xiu Xiu some water, which she uses to try to clean herself. The motorbike man has given her an apple.

More men come to Xiu Xiu for sex. She tells Lao Jin that these people who visit her are very important; she needs them, because if you want to get back to Chengdu, "you need these people on your side, stamping documents, writing permits." She asks what else she can do without connections. Lao Jin says that he can take her to the railroad so that Xiu Xiu can go back to Chengdu herself. She argues that without the proper documents, she cannot get a legal residence in Chengdu; the neighborhood committee could send her back.

Late one night, a man on a tractor arrives for Xiu Xiu. This is more than Lao Jin can stand. He burns the man's shoe in the fire. Xiu Xiu has undergone a personality change. Her hair is disheveled, and she is rude and demanding to Lao Jin. Lao Jin says that she is selling herself and that it will not do any good. In a fit of anger, Xiu Xiu breaks the kaleidoscope.

Lao Jin gives Xiu Xiu a ride to the headquarters. They cannot find anyone to confront, but one person tells them that everyone is in a meeting. The Educated Youth (students who have been sent down) are rioting. When men who have used Xiu Xiu emerge from the meeting, they pretend not to recognize her. Lao Jin threatens to shoot them; Xiu Xiu faints.

The next scene takes place in the maternity ward of a clinic or hospital. Two nurses are tending to Xiu Xiu, but not very sympathetically. She is bleeding severely; they wonder how she could do that to herself. They announce that this is the fifth girl this week in this condition. In a corner, soldiers are playing cards. One (called Three Toes) is accused of shooting himself in the foot in order to get a residence permit for Chengdu. When Three Toes goes into Xiu Xiu's room, Lao Jin attacks the soldiers and drives them away from her room. In the middle of the night, Lao Jin awakes to find that Xiu Xiu is gone. He finds her outside in the snow, and he brings her back with him to his tent.

Xiu Xiu has decided that she needs to shoot herself in the foot like Three Toes to get sent back to Chengdu. However, she can't bring herself to do it. She also realizes that it will not work. She begs Lao Jin to shoot her, saying that he is the only one who can help her; no one else will. Just before he fires, she says "Wait." She braids her hair and ties her scarf around her neck so that she looks like the schoolgirl she was when she first arrived. Lao Jin kills Xiu Xiu, then lays her in the bath he has made for her. A second shot sounds, and the bath is shown in the snow. It is clear that Lao Jin has shot himself beside Xiu Xiu.

The film ends with a voice-over by Xiu Xiu's Chengdu boyfriend saying that although her life was short, she lives on through her story.

IDEAS FOR CLASS DISCUSSION

This is a poignant story, but one that aptly illustrates the tragedy of the Cultural Revolution. There was a general breakdown of society and traditional morals during this period. An excellent resource to use with this film in the study of twentieth-century China is *Wild Swans* by Jung Chang. This is the true story of three generations of Chinese women. Chang's mother was an active member of the Communist Party, but she was denounced during the Cultural Revolution (for no apparent reason other than jealousy of various local officials). Chang herself was "sent down" from Chengdu in 1969, when every middle school in the city was closed and students were sent to remote rural areas to be reeducated by the peasants. One of Mao's sayings, cited in Chang's book, is "Peasants have dirty hands and cow-shit-sodden feet, but they are much cleaner than intellectuals." You might find it worthwhile to lead a discussion about what Mao was attempting to accomplish and why this nearly destroyed Chinese society.

BOOKS AND MATERIALS RELATING TO THIS FILM AND TOPIC

Bo, Ma. *Blood Red Sunset: A Memoir of the Chinese Cultural Revolution* (Penquin, 1996).

Chang, Jung. *The Wild Swans: Three Daughters of China* (Anchor World Views, 1992).

Dittmer, Lowell. *Liu Shaoqui and the Chinese Cultural Revolution* (M.E. Sharpe, 1998).

Salzman, Mark. *Iron and Silk: A Young American Encounters Swordsmen, Bureaucrats, and Other Citizens of Contemporary China* (Random House, 1987).

OTHER MEDIA RESOURCES FOR THIS TIME PERIOD

Animal Farm (1999, 89 minutes) A new version with live action and animatronics, this film has a rather controversial new ending that reflects the fall of Communism.

Antonia (1995, 102 minutes) In a small Dutch village, a family matriarch reflects back on her life and her family history. Rated **R**

The Burning Season (1994, 123 minutes) Raul Julia plays the part of Chico Mendes in this true story of an activist who spoke out against the destruction of the Amazon rain forest.

Cry Freedom (1987, 157 minutes) Richard Attenborough's film portrays South African activist Stephen Biko, who died while in police custody.

Kundun (1997, 128 minutes) This movie tells about the life of the 14th Dalai Lama through the Chinese invasion and his escape to India.

Local Hero (1983, 111 minutes) A major corporation runs into a stumbling block to its desire for oil rights in a small Scottish village. This film is useful in the discussion of environmental issues.

Lumumba (2000, 115 minutes) This French film tells the story of the Congo's first post-independence premier and his betrayal by Belgian and American interests.

Mandela and DeKlerk (1993, 114 minutes) This made-for-television movie is the story of the leaders who worked together to rid South Africa of apartheid; starring Sidney Poitier and Michael Caine.

Monsoon Wedding (2002, 114 minutes) A family gathers from around the world for an arranged marriage in India. This film provides good insights into traditional values that conflict with an increasingly global outlook. Rated **R**

My Beautiful Launderette (1985, 97 minutes) This film, set in an Asian community in London during the Thatcher administration, features an upwardly mobile Pakistani who wishes to have it all. Rated **R**

Not One Less (1999, 106 minutes) Recommended for younger viewers, this film tells the story of a 13-year-old girl who is assigned to teach in her village school when the schoolmaster is called away. She is given one piece of chalk for each day the teacher will be gone and is instructed to keep every single student in school. In Chinese with English subtitles.

One Day in the Life of Ivan Denisovich (1971, 105 minutes) Set in the 1950s and based on Aleksandr Solzhenitsyn's novel of the same name, this film offers a bleak look at life in a Stalinist labor camp.

The Quiet American (2002, 100 minutes) Based on the Graham Greene novel with the same title, this love triangle is set in 1950s-era Vietnam and depicts the increasing U.S. involvement in that country. Rated **R**

Raid on Entebbe (1977, 150 minutes) Israeli commandos free 103 passengers from a French airliner in Uganda, where they have been held hostage by PLO terrorists. The film is based on a true event.

Rising Sun (1993, 125 minutes) Many movies about the world at the end of the twentieth century are adventure films, involving high tech and global finance. This movie, based on a Michael Crichton novel, is typical of that genre. It features Sean Connery and Wesley Snipes in a story about a Japanese company and a U.S. defense contractor. Rated **R**

The Scent of Green Papaya (1993, 103 minutes) Set in Vietnam from 1940 to 1960, this film evokes the atmosphere of that country and its culture.

2001: A Space Odyssey (1968, 139 minutes) This is a classic film about the future and the dangers of people's overreliance on technology.

The Year of Living Dangerously (1982, 117 minutes) Mel Gibson plays the main character, a journalist in Indonesia during the upheaval of the Sukarno administration.

Z (1969, 127 minutes) This film, which is based on a true story, examines political corruption and assassination in Greece.

The End of the Twentieth Century

XIU XIU: THE SENT DOWN GIRL

Whispering Steppes LP Productions, 1998; directed by Joan Chen

Major Character	Actor/Actress
Wenxiu (Xiu Xiu)	Lu Lu
Lao Jin	Lopsang
Li Chuanbei	Zheng Qian
Mother	Jie Gao
Sister	Qianquian Li
Father	Yue Lu
Peddler	Jiangchi Min
Chen Li	Qian Qiao

WHAT TO WATCH FOR

In 1966, Mao Zedong began his Cultural Revolution in China. He planned to create a new generation of Chinese citizens with communist ideals. Communist Party members were purged, schools were closed, and intellectuals were persecuted. An attempt was made to destroy all traces of middle-class (or *bourgeois*) society and culture. As young people flocked to join Mao's Red Guard, they were allowed to demolish the old system by force. Often, the Red Guard became almost uncontrollable, as young men and women turned on their own relatives and friends. They also brutalized government officials and their former teachers.

As part of the restructuring of Chinese society, millions of young people were "sent down" from the cities to rural areas to be reeducated by the peasants. Mao thought that the peasants were the true revolutionary proletariat (working class), who were purer in thought than intellectuals and city dwellers. The peasants often treated the sent down youth with hostility and contempt. Many young people

(continued)

disappeared, never to be heard from again. Many others found that they could not return to their homes.

Director Joan Chen based her film on a novella about a 15-year-old schoolgirl named Wenxiu (Xiu Xiu). She is sent down from the provincial city of Chengdu to learn about horsemanship on the Tibetan steppes. Even though the story is fiction, the circumstances are not. Note the examples of political corruption in this story, and observe how Xiu Xiu becomes a victim of Mao's misguided ideas. Note also the complex bureaucracy of Communist China and the documents needed to move from one place to another. Residents of democratic nations tend to take the freedom to travel and live where they wish for granted. In many countries, however, special permits are necessary for these privileges.

The men who take advantage of Xiu Xiu's naïveté have no names. In the credits they are listed as Peddler or Motorcycle Man or Tractor Man. They are portrayed as totally impersonal, demonstrating even further the breakdown of the traditional Chinese community. Note also the changes in Xiu Xiu's personality and appearance throughout the film. Remember that she is just 15 years old when she is sent down. This was not unusual during the Cultural Revolution in China. Middle schools from entire cities were closed down, and the students sent away to the countryside, during this era of brutal reform.

This film has been banned in China, partly for its sexual content, but more for its obvious political statements. The director was able to film on location in China only because she used very remote sites away from government officials. Chen was fined heavily for filming without governmental permission. She has also been told that she is not welcome in China, even though she was a very popular actress in that country before she emigrated to the United States.

The End of the Twentieth Century

— *XIU XIU: THE SENT DOWN GIRL* —

VOCABULARY

Cultural Revolution   "sent down"

Red Guards   Tibet

QUESTIONS BASED ON THE FILM

1. How do Wenxiu (Xiu Xiu) and her friends view their being "sent down" to the country at the beginning of the film? What is their departure like?

   _____

   _____

   _____

2. What happens to Xiu Xiu's best friend, Chen Li?

   _____

   _____

   _____

3. Why is Xiu Xiu sent to live with Lao Jin? What skills does he have?

   _____

   _____

   _____

(continued)

4. Why can't Xiu Xiu simply go back to Chengdu on her own?

_____

_____

_____

5. What appearance and personality changes does Xiu Xiu go through during the film?

_____

_____

_____

6. How is Xiu Xiu treated at the hospital? Are the nurses sympathetic to her?

_____

_____

_____

7. How does Three Toes connive to get sent back to Chengdu?

_____

_____

8. How does this film show the bureaucracy and corruption in China during the Cultural Revolution?

_____

_____

_____

Film Analysis Guide Sheet

1. Title of the film _____

2. Date of production _____

3. Studio _____

4. Director _____

5. **Major Character**   **Actor/Actress**

   _____   _____

   _____   _____

   _____   _____

   _____   _____

   _____   _____

   _____   _____

   _____   _____

   _____   _____

   _____   _____

6. Historical event portrayed by the film _____

7. Approximate dates covered by the film _____

8. Are any historical consultants listed in the credits? If so, who? _____

   _____

   _____

(continued)

9. Synopsis of the plot _____

_____

_____

_____

10. Does this film portray the historical event or time period accurately? If so, how? (Note costuming, sets, scenery, props, manners, etc.)

_____

_____

_____

_____

11. How does this film deviate from historical facts, or, in other words, what inaccuracies can you find in this film?

_____

_____

_____

_____

12. What cinematic devices (fades, dissolves, flashbacks, montages, split scenes, bridging shots, etc.) did the filmmaker use to convey a meaning or feeling in this film? Give examples.

_____

_____

_____

_____

(continued)

Film Analysis Guide Sheet *(continued)*

13. What underlying message(s) does this film contain? Explain.

_____

_____

_____

_____

14. In your opinion, of what use is this film in explaining or illuminating a historical event, figure, or time period?

_____

_____

_____

_____

15. Research a particular aspect of the film. How does the historical research and evidence support or conflict with the film? Why do you think the filmmaker(s) chose this particular portrayal? If you were making the film, how would you stage it? Why?

_____

_____

_____

_____

_____

_____

_____

This English text of the Wannsee Protocol is based on the official U.S. government translation prepared for evidence in trials at Nuremberg, as reproduced in John Mendelsohn, ed., *The Holocaust: Selected Documents in Eighteen Volumes.* Vol. 11: *The Wannsee Protocol and a 1944 Report on Auschwitz by the Office of Strategic Services* (New York: Garland, 1982), 18–32. Substantial revisions to the Nuremberg text have been made to add clarity and, in some cases, to correct mistakes in an obviously hasty translation. These revisions were made by Dan Rogers of the University of South Alabama.

Stamp: Top Secret
30 Copies
16th copy
Minutes of discussion

I.

The following persons took part in the discussion about the final solution of the Jewish question which took place in Berlin, am Grossen Wannsee No. 56/58 on 20 January 1942.

Gauleiter Dr. Meyer and Reichsamtleiter Dr. Leibbrandt—Reich Ministry for the Occupied Eastern Territories

Secretary of State Dr. Stuckart—Reich Ministry for the Interior

Secretary of State Neumann—Plenipotentiary for the Four Year Plan

Secretary of State Dr. Freisler—Reich Ministry of Justice

Secretary of State Dr. Buehler—Office of the Government General

Under Secretary of State Dr. Luther—Foreign Office

SS-Oberfuehrer Klopfer—Party Chancellery

Ministerialdirektor Kritzinger—Reich Chancellery

SS-Gruppenfuehrer Hofmann—Race and Settlement Main Office

SS-Gruppenfuehrer Mueller and SS-Obersturmbannfuehrer Eichmann—Reich Main Security Office

SS-Oberfuehrer Dr. Schoengarth, Chief of the Security Police and the SD in the Government General—Security Police and SD

SS-Sturmbannfuehrer Dr. Lange, Commander of the Security Police and the SD for the General-District Latvia, as deputy of the Commander of the Security Police and the SD for the Reich Commissariat "Eastland"—Security Police and SD

II.

At the beginning of the discussion Chief of the Security Police and of the SD, SS-Obergruppenfuehrer Heydrich, reported that the Reich Marshal had appointed him delegate for the preparations for the final solution of the Jewish question in Europe and pointed out that this discussion had been called for the purpose of clarifying fundamental questions. The wish of the Reich Marshal to have a draft sent to him concerning organizational, factual and material interests in relation to the final solution of the Jewish question in Europe makes necessary an initial common action of all central offices immediately concerned with these questions in order to bring their general activities into line.

The Reichsfuehrer-SS and the Chief of the German Police (Chief of the Security Police and the SD) was entrusted with the official central handling of the final solution of the Jewish question without regard to geographic borders.

The chief of the Security Police and the SD then gave a short report of the struggle which has been carried on thus far against this enemy, the essential points being the following:

a) the expulsion of the Jews from every sphere of life of the German people,

b) the expulsion of the Jews from the living space of the German people.

In carrying out these efforts, an increased and planned acceleration of the emigration of the Jews from Reich territory was started, as the only possible present solution.

By order of the Reich Marshal, a Reich Central Office for Jewish Emigration was set up in January 1939 and the Chief of the Security Police and SD was entrusted with the management. Its most important tasks were

a) to make all necessary arrangements for the preparation for an increased emigration of the Jews,

b) to direct the flow of emigration,

(continued)

c) to speed the procedure of emigration in each individual case.

The aim of all this was to cleanse German living space of Jews in a legal manner.

All the offices realized the drawbacks of such enforced accelerated emigration. For the time being they had, however, tolerated it on account of the lack of other possible solutions of the problem.

The work concerned with emigration was, later on, not only a German problem, but also a problem with which the authorities of the countries to which the flow of emigrants was being directed would have to deal. Financial difficulties, such as the demand by various foreign governments for increasing sums of money to be presented at the time of the landing, the lack of shipping space, increasing restriction of entry permits, or the cancelling of such, increased extraordinarily the difficulties of emigration. In spite of these difficulties, 537,000 Jews were sent out of the country between the takeover of power and the deadline of 31 October 1941. Of these

> approximately 360,000 were in Germany proper on 30 January 1933
>
> approximately 147,000 were in Austria (Ostmark) on 15 March 1939
>
> approximately 30,000 were in the Protectorate of Bohemia and Moravia on 15 March 1939.

The Jews themselves, or their Jewish political organizations, financed the emigration. In order to avoid impoverished Jews' remaining behind, the principle was followed that wealthy Jews have to finance the emigration of poor Jews; this was arranged by imposing a suitable tax, i.e., an emigration tax, which was used for financial arrangements in connection with the emigration of poor Jews and was imposed according to income.

Apart from the necessary Reichsmark exchange, foreign currency had to presented at the time of landing. In order to save forcign exchange held by Germany, the foreign Jewish financial organizations were—with the help of Jewish organizations in Germany—made responsible for arranging an adequate amount of foreign currency. Up to 30 October 1941, these foreign Jews donated a total of around 9,500,000 dollars.

In the meantime the Reichsfuehrer-SS and Chief of the German Police had prohibited emigration of Jews due to the dangers of an emigration in wartime and due to the possibilities of the East.

III.

Another possible solution of the problem has now taken the place of emigration, i.e. the evacuation of the Jews to the East, provided that the Fuehrer gives the appropriate approval in advance.

These actions are, however, only to be considered provisional, but practical experience is already being collected which is of the greatest importance in relation to the future final solution of the Jewish question.

Approximately 11 million Jews will be involved in the final solution of the European Jewish question, distributed as follows among the individual countries:

COUNTRY	NUMBER
A.	
Germany proper	131,800
Austria	43,700
Eastern territories	420,000
General Government	2,284,000
Bialystok	400,000
Protectorate Bohemia and Moravia	74,200
Estonia	free of Jews
Latvia	3,500
Lithuania	34,000
Belgium	43,000
Denmark	5,600
France/occupied territory	165,000
unoccupied territory	700,000
Greece	69,600
Netherlands	160,800
Norway	1,300
B.	
Bulgaria	48,000
England	330,000
Finland	2,300
Ireland	4,000
Italy including Sardinia	58,000
Albania	200
Croatia	40,000
Portugal	3,000
Rumania including Bessarabia	342,000
Sweden	8,000

(continued)

Switzerland	18,000
Serbia	10,000
Slovakia	88,000
Spain	6,000
Turkey (European portion)	55,500
Hungary	742,800
USSR	5,000,000
Ukraine	2,994,684
White Russia, excluding Bialystok	446,484
Total	over 11,000,000

The number of Jews given here for foreign countries includes, however, only those Jews who still adhere to the Jewish faith, since some countries still do not have a definition of the term "Jew" according to racial principles.

The handling of the problem in the individual countries will meet with difficulties due to the attitude and outlook of the people there, especially in Hungary and Rumania. Thus, for example, even today the Jew can buy documents in Rumania that will officially prove his foreign citizenship.

The influence of the Jews in all walks of life in the USSR is well known. Approximately five million Jews live in the European part of the USSR, in the Asian part scarcely $\frac{1}{4}$ million.

The breakdown of Jews residing in the European part of the USSR according to trades was approximately as follows:

Agriculture	9.1 %
Urban workers	14.8 %
In trade	20.0 %
Employed by the state	23.4 %
In private occupations such as medical profession, press, theater, etc.	32.7%

Under proper guidance, in the course of the final solution the Jews are to be allocated for appropriate labor in the East. Able-bodied Jews, separated according to sex, will be taken in large work columns to these areas for work on roads, in the course of which action doubtless a large portion will be eliminated by natural causes.

The possible final remnant will, since it will undoubtedly consist of the most resistant portion, have to be treated accordingly, because it is the product of natural selection and would, if released, act as the seed of a new Jewish revival (see the experience of history.)

In the course of the practical execution of the final solution, Europe will be combed through from west to east. Germany proper, including the Protectorate of Bohemia and Moravia, will have to be handled first due to the housing problem and additional social and political necessities.

The evacuated Jews will first be sent, group by group, to so-called transit ghettos, from which they will be transported to the East.

SS-Obergruppenfuehrer Heydrich went on to say that an important prerequisite for the evacuation as such is the exact definition of the persons involved.

It is not intended to evacuate Jews over 65 years old, but to send them to an old-age ghetto—Theresienstadt is being considered for this purpose.

In addition to these age groups—of the approximately 280,000 Jews in Germany proper and Austria on 31 October 1941, approximately 30% are over 65 years old—severely wounded veterans and Jews with war decorations (Iron Cross I) will be accepted in the old-age ghettos. With this expedient solution, in one fell swoop many interventions will be prevented.

The beginning of the individual larger evacuation actions will largely depend on military developments. Regarding the handling of the final solution in those European countries occupied and influenced by us, it was proposed that the appropriate expert of the Foreign Office discuss the matter with the responsible official of the Security Police and SD.

In Slovakia and Croatia the matter is no longer so difficult, since the most substantial problems in this respect have already been brought near a solution. In Rumania the government has in the meantime also appointed a commissioner for Jewish affairs. In order to settle the question in Hungary, it will soon be necessary to force an adviser for Jewish questions onto the Hungarian government.

With regard to taking up preparations for dealing with the problem in Italy, SS-Obergruppenfuehrer Heydrich considers it opportune to contact the chief of police with a view to these problems.

In occupied and unoccupied France, the registration of Jews for evacuation will in all probability proceed without great difficulty.

Under Secretary of State Luther calls attention in this matter to the fact that in some countries, such as the Scandinavian states, difficulties will arise if this problem is dealt with thoroughly and that it will therefore be advisable to defer actions in these countries. Besides, in view of the small numbers of Jews affected, this deferral will not cause any substantial limitation.

The Foreign Office sees no great difficulties for southeast and western Europe.

(continued)

SS-Gruppenfuehrer Hofmann plans to send an expert to Hungary from the Race and Settlement Main Office for general orientation at the time when the Chief of the Security Police and SD takes up the matter there. It was decided to assign this expert from the Race and Settlement Main Office, who will not work actively, as an assistant to the police attache.

IV.

In the course of the final solution plans, the Nuremberg Laws should provide a certain foundation, in which a prerequisite for the absolute solution of the problem is also the solution to the problem of mixed marriages and persons of mixed blood.

The Chief of the Security Police and the SD discusses the following points, at first theoretically, in regard to a letter from the chief of the Reich chancellery:

1) Treatment of Persons of Mixed Blood of the First Degree

    Persons of mixed blood of the first degree will, as regards the final solution of the Jewish question, be treated as Jews.

    From this treatment the following exceptions will be made:

    a) Persons of mixed blood of the first degree married to persons of German blood if their marriage has resulted in children (persons of mixed blood of the second degree). These persons of mixed blood of the second degree are to be treated essentially as Germans.

    b) Persons of mixed blood of the first degree, for whom the highest offices of the Party and State have already issued exemption permits in any sphere of life. Each individual case must be examined, and it is not ruled out that the decision may be made to the detriment of the person of mixed blood.

    The prerequisite for any exemption must always be the personal merit of the person of mixed blood. (Not the merit of the parent or spouse of German blood.)

    Persons of mixed blood of the first degree who are exempted from evacuation will be sterilized in order to prevent any offspring and to eliminate the problem of persons of mixed blood once and for all. Such sterilization will be voluntary. But it is required to remain in the Reich. The sterilized "person of mixed blood" is thereafter free of all restrictions to which he was previously subjected.

2) Treatment of Persons of Mixed Blood of the Second Degree

    Persons of mixed blood of the second degree will be treated fundamentally as persons of German blood, with the exception of the following cases, in which the persons of mixed blood of the second degree will be considered as Jews:

    a) The person of mixed blood of the second degree was born of a marriage in which both parents are persons of mixed blood.

    b) The person of mixed blood of the second degree has a racially especially undesirable appearance that marks him outwardly as a Jew.

    c) The person of mixed blood of the second degree has a particularly bad police and political record that shows that he feels and behaves like a Jew.

    Also in these cases exemptions should not be made if the person of mixed blood of the second degree has married a person of German blood.

3) Marriages between Full Jews and Persons of German Blood

    Here it must be decided from case to case whether the Jewish partner will be evacuated or whether, with regard to the effects of such a step on the German relatives, [this mixed marriage] should be sent to an old-age ghetto.

4) Marriages between Persons of Mixed Blood of the First Degree and Persons of German Blood

    a) Without Children

    If no children have resulted from the marriage, the person of mixed blood of the first degree will be evacuated or sent to an old-age ghetto (same treatment as in the case of marriages between full Jews and persons of German blood, point 3).

    b) With Children

    If children have resulted from the marriage (persons of mixed blood of the second degree), they will, if they are to be treated as Jews, be evacuated or sent to a ghetto along with the parent of mixed blood of the first degree. If these children are to be treated as Germans (regular cases), they are exempted from evacuation as is therefore the parent of mixed blood of the first degree.

5) Marriages between Persons of Mixed Blood of the First Degree and Persons of Mixed Blood of the First Degree or Jews

(continued)

In these marriages (including the children) all members of the family will be treated as Jews and therefore be evacuated or sent to an old-age ghetto.

6) Marriages between Persons of Mixed Blood of the First Degree and Persons of Mixed Blood of the Second Degree

In these marriages both partners will be evacuated or sent to an old-age ghetto without consideration of whether the marriage has produced children, since possible children will as a rule have stronger Jewish blood than the Jewish person of mixed blood of the second degree.

SS-Gruppenfuehrer Hofmann advocates the opinion that sterilization will have to be widely used, since the person of mixed blood who is given the choice whether he will be evacuated or sterilized would rather undergo sterilization.

State Secretary Dr. Stuckart maintains that carrying out in practice of the just mentioned possibilities for solving the problem of mixed marriages and persons of mixed blood will create endless administrative work. In the second place, as the biological facts cannot be disregarded in any case, State Secretary Dr. Stuckart proposed proceeding to forced sterilization.

Furthermore, to simplify the problem of mixed marriages possibilities must be considered with the goal of the legislator saying something like: "These marriages have been dissolved."

With regard to the issue of the effect of the evacuation of Jews on the economy, State Secretary Neumann stated that Jews who are working in industries vital to the war effort, provided that no replacements are available, cannot be evacuated.

SS-Obergruppenfuehrer Heydrich indicated that these Jews would not be evacuated according to the rules he had approved for carrying out the evacuations then underway.

State Secretary Dr. Buehler stated that the General Government would welcome it if the final solution of this problem could be begun in the General Government, since on the one hand transportation does not play such a large role here nor would problems of labor supply hamper this action. Jews must be removed from the territory of the General Government as quickly as possible, since it is especially here that the Jew as an epidemic carrier represents an extreme danger and on the other hand he is causing permanent chaos in the economic structure of the country through continued black market dealings. Moreover, of the approximately $2\frac{1}{2}$ million Jews concerned, the majority is unfit for work.

State Secretary Dr. Buehler stated further that the solution to the Jewish question in the General Government is the responsibility of the Chief of the Security Police and the SD and that his efforts would be supported by the officials of the General Government. He had only one request, to solve the Jewish question in this area as quickly as possible.

In conclusion the different types of possible solutions were discussed, during which discussion both Gauleiter Dr. Meyer and State Secretary Dr. Buehler took the position that certain preparatory activities for the final solution should be carried out immediately in the territories in question, in which process alarming the populace must be avoided.

The meeting was closed with the request of the Chief of the Security Police and the SD to the participants that they afford him appropriate support during the carrying out of the tasks involved in the solution.

Glossary of Common Film Terms

actuality footage: film or video that is not set up and/or dramatized; e.g., newsreel film

aspect ratio: the ratio of the horizontal to the vertical in television or film; film has an aspect ratio of 6 horizontal units to 4 vertical units, while television has an aspect ratio of 4 to 3. This is what necessitates letter-boxing a film to make it fit a television screen without distortion.

audio: the sound in a film or broadcast

backlighting: using the main source of light behind a subject to silhouette the figure

black comedy: comedy that deals with macabre topics such as murder or nuclear war; *Dr. Strangelove* is a good example.

bridging shot: shot that covers a jump in place or time, such as newspaper headlines, falling leaves, hands of a clock, or an airplane taking off

camera angle: angle at which a camera is pointed at a subject; a high-angle shot from above a subject can make the subject look small. A low-angle shot can make a subject look large.

cinematography: the art and science of motion picture photography; *videography* is a term used to describe video photography.

close-up: any close shot, usually of a subject's face

credits: the list, usually at the end of a film, of the crew and cast of a production

cut: the instantaneous switch from one image or scene to another

crosscutting: cutting between two or more scenes to portray parallel action —events that are occurring simultaneously

dissolve: to fade out one image while fading in another

docudramas: historical events that are reenacted, often in fictionalized versions; for example, *Roots, Holocaust*

documentary: film that is generally, but not always or completely, nonfictional, usually containing actuality footage, interviews, and a narration; *documentary* is an elastic term that may include reenactments, still pictures, sound effects, stock footage, graphics, and/or interpretive materials.

dolly shot: shot taken with a camera moving on wheels (called a dolly); also called a follow or tracking shot

DVD: digital video disc; more and more films are coming out on DVD, which gives a clearer image and allows the viewer to access certain parts of the films without forwarding and rewinding.

editor: the person who cuts and splices together the film into its final form; editors in video do this electronically with computerized equipment.

establishing shot: a wide shot that establishes the location of a scene for the viewer

fade-in/-out: In a fade-in, the screen gradually changes from black to the image. In a fade-out, the image dissolves to black.

flashback: a scene that is brought into the film from the past; sometimes almost an entire film can be a flashback from the present to the past, as in *Little Big Man.*

focus: the clarity or sharpness of an image

(continued)

foley: a largely manual process for introducing any nonmusical or nonspoken sound effect or noise as part of the postproduction process

freeze frame: stopping of an individual frame to give the impression of a still image or photograph

gaffer: the chief electrician in a production; the *best boy* is the gaffer's assistant.

genre: the type of a film, such as science fiction, Western, or horror film

grip: the person in charge of props, sometimes called the key grip

letter boxing: the technique of compressing a film horizontally and enclosing it in black on the top and bottom of the screen to make it fit on a television screen without distortion

mise-en-scène: what actually takes place on the set—the actors, direction, type of cameras, etc.

montage: (1) the editing of film; (2) editing shots together in such a way as to produce a total meaning different from the parts actually shown

narrative: the story of a film

over-the-shoulder shot: shot used in interviews or dialogue in which the camera is placed behind and to the side of one of the speakers to show a portion of his or her head and shoulders as well as the other speaker

pan: the horizontal movement of the camera lens from left to right or right to left

pan and scan: In a film produced on DVD for use on a consumer television set, to show the reactions of two main characters who may be standing far apart from each other, a technique is used where first a close-up of one and then a close-up of the other is shown superimposed over the scene. This is to compensate for the small screen on a television set and its smaller aspect ratio.

point-of-view shot: also called a subjective shot, a shot that shows the scene from the point of view of one of the subjects

reverse angle: a shot taken from the opposite side of a subject from that previously shown, often to show a second person in a dialogue

scene: a coherent segment of the film, made up of a number of shots, that takes place in one location and at one time period and usually revolves around one particular action

sequence: a section of film containing a group of scenes that constitutes a more or less complete thought, very often beginning and ending with a cut, dissolve, or fade

shot: a single unedited piece of film or video that is taken by a camera

split screen: section of film with two or more distinct images on the screen that are not superimposed and do not overlap

stock footage: film or video shot for one purpose but used for another, usually used as background or establishing material

tilt: the vertical movement of the camera lens up and down

videography: See cinematography.

voice-over: narration in which the narrator is not seen, used often in documentaries and television commercials

wipe: an effect where one image pushes or "wipes" another image off the screen; wipes can have many shapes and are used more in television than in film.

zoom: changing the focal length using the special lens of the camera to go from wide angle to telephoto or vice versa

Video Sources

A&E Home Video, P.O. Box 2284, South Burlington,
VT 05407. 800-344-6336 (FAX 802-864-9846)
www.AandE.com

Ambrose Video Publishing, Inc., 145 W. 45th St.,
Suite 1115, New York, NY 10036.
800-526-4663 (FAX 212-768-9282)
www.ambrosevideo.com

Facets Multimedia, 1517 W. Fullerton Avenue,
Chicago, IL 60614. 800-331-6197
www.facets.org

Films for the Humanities, P.O. Box 2053, Princeton,
NJ 08543-2053. 800-257-5126
www.films.com

History Channel (see A&E Home Video)
www.historychannel.com

International Historic Films, Inc.,
P.O. Box 29035, Chicago, IL 60629.
773-927-2900 (FAX 773-927-9211)
www.ihffilm.com

Kino Video, 333 W. 39th St., Suite 503, New York, NY
10014. 800-562-3330 (FAX 212-714-0871)
www.kino.com

Metropolitan Museum of Art, 1000 Fifth Avenue,
New York, NY 10028. 212-879-5500
(FAX 212-472-8725)
www.metmuseum.org

Movies Unlimited, 3015 Darnell Road, Philadelphia,
PA 19154. 800-668-4344
www.moviesunlimited.com

National Archives, National Audiovisual Center,
8700 Edgeworth Drive, Capitol Heights, MD
20743-3701

New Yorker Video, 16 W. 61st Street, New York, NY
10023. 877-247-6200, 212-247-6110
www.newyorkerfilms.com

PBS Video/Customer Support Center,
1320 Braddock Place, Alexandria, VA 22314-1698.
800-344-3337 (FAX 703-739-5269)
www.pbs.org

SVE & Churchill Media, 6677 N. Northwest Highway,
Chicago, IL 60631. 800-253-2788
(FAX 800-624-1678)
www.svemedia.com

Teacher's Video Company, P.O. Box 4455-02AH03,
Scottsdale, AZ 85261. 800-262-8837
www.teachersvideo.com

Video Yesteryear, Box C, Sandy Hook, CT 06482-
0847. 800-243-0987

Zenger Media, 10200 Jefferson Blvd., P.O. Box 802,
Culver City, CA 90232-0802. 800-421-4246
(FAX 800-944-5432)
www.zengermedia.com

Media-Related Web Sites

FEATURE FILM AND VIDEO INFORMATION

*Internet Movie Database: **www.imdb.com**

Movie Studios: **www.cs.duke.edu/~fan/ movies/makers.html**

*Northwestern University Library: "I Saw It on TV . . .": **www.library.northwestern. edu/media/resources/tvguide/ tvpubbroad.htm**

TV Guide Entertainment Network: **www.tvguide.com**

Yahoo! Movies and Films: **dir.yahoo.com/ Entertainment/Movies_and_Film**

* best sites

ACADEMIC/DOCUMENTARY FILM AND VIDEO

Docuseek Film and Video Finder: **www.docuseek.com**

Media Reference and Links: **www.lib. berkeley.edu/MRC/mediarefmenu.html**

*Media Resource Center, University of California, Berkeley: **www.lib.berkeley.edu/MRC/ level2.html**

NICEM AV Producer/Distributor Archive: **www.nicem.com/pdurl.htm**

*PBS Online: **www.pbs.org**

Video University (Guide to Public Domain Footage): **www.videouniversity.com**

* best sites

REVIEWS

American Libraries: Quick Vids**: **www.lib.berkeley.edu/MRC/quickvids. html**

Booklist**: **www.ala.org/booklist/v96/003. html**

Bright Lights Film Journal: **www.brightlightsfilm.com**

Educational Media Reviews Online**: **libweb.lib.buffalo.edu/emro/search.html**

Inside Out (United Kingdom): **www.iofilm.co.uk**

*MC Journal: The Journal of Academic Media Librarianship**: **wings.buffalo.edu/ publications/mcjrnl**

*MRQE: Movie Review Query Engine: **www.mrqe.com**

*Roger Ebert on Movies: **suntimes.com/ebert/ebert.html**

Rotten Tomatoes: **www.rottentomatoes.com**

Variety: **www.variety.com**

Video Librarian OnLine**: **www.videolibrarian.com**

* best sites

**academic/documentary titles

(continued)

Media-Related Web Sites *(continued)*

FILM HISTORY AND RESEARCH

American Film Institute: **www.afi.com**

*National Film Preservation Foundation:
www.filmpreservation.org

News Film Archive at University of South Carolina:
www.sc.edu/newsfilm

Public Moving Images Archives and Research
Centers: **lcweb.loc.gov/film/arch.html**

UCLA Film and Television Archive:
www.cinema.ucla.edu

* best site

COPYRIGHT ISSUES

Copyright Bay: **www.stfrancis.edu/cid/
copyrightbay**

Copyright and Fair Use: **fairuse.stanford.edu**

*The Copyright Website: **www.benedict.com**

U.S. Copyright Office: **lcweb.loc.gov/copyright**

* best site

Bibliography

GUIDES TO MEDIA USE

Carnes, Mark C., ed. *Past Imperfect: History According to the Movies.* New York: Owl/Henry Holt, 1996.

Edgerton, Gary R., and Peter C. Rollins. *Television Histories: Shaping Collective Memory in the Media Age.* Lexington, KY: University Press of Kentucky, 2000.

Fraser, George MacDonald. *The Hollywood History of the World.* New York: Beechtree Books, 1988.

Furtaw, Julia C., ed. *The Video Source Book.* Detroit: Gale Research Inc., 1993.

Harty, Kevin J. *The Reel Middle Ages: American, Western and Eastern European, Middle Eastern, and Asian Films About Medieval Europe.* Jefferson, NC: McFarland & Company, 1999.

Klossner, Michael. *The Europe of 1500–1815 on Film and Television: A Worldwide Filmography of Over 2,550 Works, 1895 Through 2000.* Jefferson, NC: McFarland & Company, 2002.

Lacey, Richard. *Seeing with Feeling: Film in the Classroom.* Philadelphia: Saunders, 1972.

Maynard, Richard A. *The Celluloid Curriculum: How to Use Movies in the Classroom.* New York: Hayden Books, 1971.

Mitchell, Charles P. *The Hitler Filmography: Worldwide Feature Film and Television Miniseries Portrayals, 1940 Through 2000.* Jefferson, NC: McFarland & Company, 2002.

Moraco, James. *How to Read a Film: The Art, Technology, Language, History, and Theory of Film and Media.* Rev. ed. New York: Oxford University Press, 1981.

O'Connor, John E. *Discussions on Teaching 2: Teaching History with Film and Television.* Washington, DC: American Historical Association, 1987.

_____, ed. *Image as Artifact: Historical Analysis of Film and Television.* Malabar, FL: Krieger, 1989.

_____, comp. *Image as Artifact: Video Compilation.* Washington, DC: American Historical Association, 1988.

Rebhorn, Marlettte. *Screening America: Using Hollywood Films to Teach History.* New York: Lang, 1989.

Rollins, Peter C., ed. *Hollywood as Historian: American Film in a Cultural Context.* Lexington, KY: University Press of Kentucky, 1983.

Rosenstone, Robert A. *Visions of the Past: The Challenge of Film to Our Idea of History.* Cambridge, MA: Harvard University Press, 1995.

_____, ed. *Revisioning History: Film and the Construction of a New Past.* Princeton, NJ: Princeton University Press, 1995.

Thomas, Tony. *Hollywood and the American Image.* Westport, CT: Arlington House, 1981.

Toplin, Robert Brent. *The Cinematic Historian: Hollywood Interprets America.* Urbana, IL: University of Illinois Press, 1984.

(continued)

_____, intro., *Perspectives on Audiovisuals in the Teaching of History: A Collection of Essays from* Perspectives, *the Newsletter of the American Historial Association.* Washington, DC: American Historical Association, 1999.

_____, *Reel History: In Defense of Hollywood.* Lawrence, KS: University Press of Kansas, 2002.

FINDER'S AIDS

Leff, Leonard J. *Film Plots: Scene-by-Scene Narrative Outlines for Feature Film Study.* 2 vols. Ann Arbor, MI: Pierian Press, 1983–88.

Maltin, Leonard. *Leonard Maltin's Movie and Video Guide.* New York: Signet, 2002. (reissued yearly)

Media Log: A Guide to Film, Television, and Radio Programs Supported by the National Endowment for the Humanities. Washington, DC: U.S. Government Printing Office, 1993.

Pratt, Douglas. *The Laser Video Disc Companion.* New York: Zoetrope, 1992.

Reed, Maxine K., ed. *The Video Source Book.* 7th ed. 2 vols. Syosset, NY: National Video Clearinghouse, 2001. (issued yearly)

Scheuer, Steven H., ed. *Movies on TV and Videocassette.* New York: Bantam, 1993. (issued yearly)

Videohound's Golden Movie Retriever. Detroit: Visible Ink Press, 2002. (updated annually)

Zaniello, Tom. *Working Stiffs, Union Maids, Reds, and Riffraff: An Organized Guide to Films About Labor.* Ithaca, NY: ILR Press, 1996.

Master Index
of Feature Films

Asterisked films are featured in depth in a unit. Other films are synopsized on the indicated page.

Unit 8: The French Revolution and Napoléon

Unit 9: The Industrial Revolution

Unit 10: Exploration: From Across the Atlantic to Outer Space

Unit 11: Imperialism

Unit 12 : World War I

Unit 13: The Russian Revolution

Unit 14 : The World Between the Wars: The Decline of Colonialism

Unit 18: The End of the Twentieth Century

About the Authors

Wendy S. Wilson has been a teacher in the Lexington, Massachusetts, public schools since 1971. She has taught social studies in grades 7–12, has been appointed interim social studies department head, and has served as the cable television specialist systemwide. She also has been a senior lecturer in history at University College, Northeastern University, since 1972; she team-teaches a graduate course on history and media with Gerald Herman as well as an undergraduate course on films of the 1930s. Wilson has been a frequent presenter at national conferences and was the only public-school teacher asked to serve on a task force titled The Historian and Moving-Image Media, which was funded by the National Endowment for the Humanities and the American Historical Association. As a program developer and on-camera presenter, she has hosted three series on an educational satellite network—two on the Columbus Quincentennial and one on U.S. immigration. Wilson is the author of several other Walch publications on social studies topics, including *American History on the Screen, Daily Warm-Ups: World History* and *Critical Thinking Using Primary Sources in U.S. History.*

Gerald H. Herman is a tenured assistant professor of history and education and a special assistant to the office of the general counsel at Northeastern University. He is the author of a nine-part multimedia presentation and anthology on the culture of World War I titled *World War I: The Destroying Fathers Confirmed* and of award-winning National Public Radio programs—one called *War* on the same subject, and another on culture of World War II called *The Sound in the Fury.* Herman also has written extensively on history and film, including analyses of individual films, teacher guides for secondary schools and colleges, and bibliographical references (including the media section of *The Craft of Public History* published by Greenwood in 1983). He currently serves as media editor for *The Public Historian.* As a media writer and producer, he created a 40-program instructional television history of Western civilization, *Windows on the Past,* and a video for the National Council on Public History, *Public History Today.* Herman recently published an extensive filmography of dramatic and documentary films about World War I in *Hollywood's World War I: Motion Picture Images* (Peter C. Rollins and John E. O'Connor, eds., Popular Press, Bowling Green State University, 1997). He is currently writing a comprehensive *Historians' Guide to Films.*

Share Your Bright Ideas

We want to hear from you!

Your name_____Date_____

School name_____

School address_____

City _____State _____Zip_____Phone number (_____)_____

Grade level(s) taught_____Subject area(s) taught_____

Where did you purchase this publication?_____

In what month do you purchase a majority of your supplements?_____

What moneys were used to purchase this product?

____School supplemental budget   ____Federal/state funding   ____Personal

Please "grade" this Walch publication in the following areas:

	A	B	C	D
Quality of service you received when purchasing	A	B	C	D
Ease of use	A	B	C	D
Quality of content	A	B	C	D
Page layout	A	B	C	D
Organization of material	A	B	C	D
Suitability for grade level	A	B	C	D
Instructional value	A	B	C	D

COMMENTS:_____

_____

What specific supplemental materials would help you meet your current—or future—instructional needs?

_____

Have you used other Walch publications? If so, which ones?_____

May we use your comments in upcoming communications?   ____Yes   ____No

Please **FAX** this completed form to **888-991-5755**, or mail it to

Customer Service, J. Weston Walch, Publisher, P. O. Box 658, Portland, ME 04104-0658

We will send you a **FREE GIFT** in appreciation of your feedback. **THANK YOU!**